Making
Miniatures
Projects for the 1:12 Scale Dolls' House

Making Miniatures

Projects for the 1:12 Scale Dolls' House

Christiane Berridge

GUILD OF
MASTER CRAFTSMAN
PUBLICATIONS

To my father, Barrie Huntbach, with much love

First published 2003 by
Guild of Master Craftsman Publications Ltd
166 High Street, Lewes
East Sussex BN7 1XU

ISBN 1 86108 381 5

British Cataloguing in Publication Data
A catalogue record of this book is available from the British Library.

Designed by GMC Publications.
Photographs: Anthony Bailey, GMC Publications Photographic Studio,
with the exception of Man in Deck Chair, p. 3: Paula Huntbach
Diagrams based on drawings by Christiane Berridge
Typefaces: Helvetica, Palatino and Shelley
Colour origination by Viscan Graphics Pte Ltd, Singapore
Printed and bound by Stamford Press Ltd (Singapore)

Contents

Introduction

*W*hen I discovered dolls' houses it was as though a locked door had been opened. Here was a hobby that united many of my existing interests and I could be creative with a purpose, indulging my love of social history, architecture, painting, making and sewing along the way.

Six years on from that initial discovery I am as excited by the subject as ever. What I love about dolls' houses and miniatures is that they are so accessible. You can buy or make, or mix and match. This is a passion that is open to all and can comfortably span the generations and my head is full of ideas that I only wish I had the time to develop.

Dolls' houses suit imperial measurements, and I am a devotee of 1:12 scale, where one inch (25mm) in miniature represents one foot (305mm) in real life. The projects in this book reflect that interest. I find it easy to work at this scale, though I am told that it's just a matter of practice converting to the half scale or 1:24, where half an inch (13mm) in miniature represents one foot (305mm) in real life. If you prefer to work in 1:24 scale, you can adapt the ideas given here to suit.

While you can choose to create a strictly accurate period dolls' house, there are no firm rules when it comes to what to do. This book shows you some projects to try, ideas to embrace, possibilities to consider, and photographs to inspire. You don't need great artistic skills, just a little time and imagination to create your own unique pieces for your dolls' house. Adapt the projects if you wish, and explore your own ideas. By doing so, each one becomes an intensely personal creation and the experience of making it will be so much more enjoyable.

But be warned – this hobby is addictive. With a dolls' house at your fingertips the creative possibilities are endless and before long you will discover that one just isn't enough.

An illustrated view of the hobby

Augusta Villa

I made this, my first dolls' house, following plans in Michal Morse's book, *Build a Dolls' House* (published by Batsford). I had the wood cut by a timber merchant, so it was just a matter of putting the pieces together like a commercial kit. I agonized over the interior, not knowing what was then commercially available, and made several mistakes during the construction.

The 'sandpaper' bricks took hours to apply to the exterior and I eventually gave up in favour of stencilling a brick effect. But I learnt a lot about the hobby from working on this house and I even went on to design and build an extension to it, to incorporate a scullery. bathroom and conservatory.

Charleston Farmhouse frame box

This scene shows that you don't need a dolls' house to indulge in miniatures. I love Charleston Farmhouse, at Firle (Southeast England), which was home to members of the artistic Bloomsbury Group. This room represents some of its elements such as the painted surfaces, the fabric design, and the literary association of Charleston's many visitors. As the contents can be personalized, frame boxes can be designed to make individual gifts to celebrate birthdays or special anniversaries.

Man in deck chair

Anything can be used to house miniatures, as this witty scene illustrates. Fabric soaked in wallpaper paste retains its shape once dried, and in this case a knotted handkerchief has been used to complement the beach scene. Sandpaper represents the shore, and buckets and spades, a windbreak, and a book to read complete the scene.

Victorian schoolroom

I was asked to make this late Victorian schoolroom
for a local museum. Schoolrooms are a popular
choice in miniature and these benches are all
made from kits. I enjoyed making the children to sit
in the classroom, although their tiny hands were
rather tricky. The schoolroom includes a number
of items to spark a debate about Victorian
education, including the pictures on the wall, the
clothes worn, and the games played. It would be
fun to turn a whole dolls' house into a miniature
boarding school.

Writer's block

This model isn't a conventional room, but it is a 1:12 scale study complete with bookcase, desk, chair and fireplace. The result resembles an art form more than a miniature. By having the books fly out from the bookcase the scene is given movement – something that is often lacking in the conventional dolls' house. This piece has been much admired as it blurs the boundary between art and architecture.

Bungalow

Basic 'tab and slot' dolls' houses are inexpensive, and useful for trying out new ideas. I covered the exterior of this house with multi-purpose filler, and stippled it to provide a textured surface. The roof tiles are made from sheets of sandpaper, which are wonderfully tactile and come in useful shades of yellow, brown and grey. New French doors have improved the façade, and adding a wider base to the dolls' house provided space for a garden.

Narnia

Stories are a great source of inspiration for miniature projects and this split scene, based on *The Chronicles of Narnia* by C. S. Lewis, was something that I had wanted to try for a long time. The project is set on a 12in (305mm) base of MDF, with a wall traversing this slightly off the centre diagonal. The central wall has a hole cut in it with a wardrobe fixed to one side. The snowy landscape is made up from scrap wood and chunks of polystyrene banked up against the wall, covered with quilt wadding to resemble snow.

Model railway shops are a good source of miniature trees in a variety of sizes. Lightly brush white paint across their branches to represent snow and push their trunks into the polystyrene with a dollop of PVA. The sparkling twigs were a lucky find in a garden centre at Christmas time.

The wallpaper on the 'home' side has been smudged with very dilute black paint to highlight the unused nature of the room. Likewise, paint has been smeared across the mirror panels in the wardrobe. This is an easy way to add atmosphere to a room.

The figures are both made from kits. I adapted one kit to create Mr Tumnus, the faun. His lower half was originally a female doll, standing as though in high heels. His top half was male. I used a modelling medium around the feet to turn the raised heels into hooves and to make the horns on his head. To clothe the faun's legs I used real fur. This was glued around the top of the legs like a pair of trousers, but padded out to form a more animal shape.

RISTMAS VARIETY

ALI BABA
AND THE
TY THIEVE

FOR

NOW
SHOWING AT
THE PALACE THEATRE
PERFORMANCES
TWICE DAILY

COME ALONG
AND SEE THE FUN

Getting started

If you haven't yet acquired your first dolls'
house, or are in the process of choosing
another, here are a few points to bear in
mind before the creative work can begin.

Basic equipment needed

The projects in this book can be made using basic equipment, including the following:

- Self-healing cutting mat
- Craft knife or scalpel, with a sharp blade
- Scissors: one pair for fabric and another dedicated to paper
- Metal ruler, marked with millimetres and inches

- PVA glue
- Wood glue
- Pencil
- Rubber
- Paintbrushes
- Masking tape

Of course, not all of these are needed for every project and some projects may require more specialist items, so always check what is needed before embarking on a project.

Sourcing a dolls' house

You can obtain dolls' houses in various ways: you can buy a commercial kit or a ready-made house from a dolls' house shop or fair; you might find a second-hand dolls' house at a bargain price; you could use commercially available plans to construct your own dolls' house – provided that you are competent at woodwork – or you could draw up your own plans. Commissioning a building can result in a unique dolls' house. There are lots of different styles of dolls' houses, so take your time looking around before making up your mind.

Before acquiring your dolls' house, think carefully about its overall dimensions and the amount of floor space it is going to take up.

Draw the base size out on newspaper and lay it out in your real house to see how it fits into its intended location. Can the dolls' house sit on top of an existing chest of drawers or table, where it might be easier to access? If you only have room for one special building these decisions are even more crucial.

Look at the individual room sizes in your prospective dolls' house – can you fit furniture in comfortably? Take a suite with you to try before you buy. Are the ceilings high enough to accommodate chandeliers? Are you happy with the period frontage of the house? Think carefully about the period detail, such as windows and doors. You may develop a passion for another era once you've seen what else is available.

Buying second-hand can produce bargains. It may also result in a unique house, particularly if you buy at auction where you might also buy a little history. But don't get carried away – it is easy to fall in love with a building and not notice the drawbacks until you get it home. Check to see how straightforward it will be to redecorate. Is the staircase removable? How difficult would it be to wallpaper that back wall? Above all, measure the dimensions carefully, to make sure that your new house will fit through your own front door.

Many dolls' houses will be made from MDF (medium density fibreboard). This material is easy to paint and is very sturdy. It is essential to wear a

△ You can decorate the exterior of your dolls' house to resemble a variety of building materials, such as brick or stone. Stippled grey, black and white acrylic paint here resembles flint. Cut-out brick paper has provided decorative courses of brickwork.

dust mask when cutting MDF, because of the toxic nature of the dust. Plywood is the other material frequently used for dolls' houses. This should be treated (painted) on both sides to prevent warping. Dolls' house makers may use a combination of materials. A real wood house can look wonderful when the exterior is just varnished.

Choosing for children

Children interact with their dolls' houses in a different way to adults, and will happily play with a cardboard box if their imagination has turned it into a house. When buying a dolls' house for a child look for one that is aimed specifically at them, rather than one for the adult collector.

The furniture and accessories on sale in dolls' house shops and at specialist fairs is aimed at the 14-year-old and above. It may look pretty but, in the hands of a small child, it will be roughly treated despite your encouragement to the reverse. Also remember that small items are easily lost (or swallowed), if not by your child then by their friends.

Children don't need architraves and skirting boards, but will appreciate opening doors and a staircase, as dolls are moved around the rooms. Don't underestimate the child's imagination to fill in the details. A dolls' house may be a home one day, a school the next, or a hospital after that. Later on a child may take more interest in what a room looks like, the furniture and accessories. There will be plenty of time to encourage this as the child grows up and becomes a discerning collector.

Look for chunky furniture – there are plenty of affordable sets available sets from retailers – or use scraps and oddments to make your own, before spending well-earned money. Cutting and sticking is a good activity for children used to the instant gratification of the television and computer screen.

This is a hobby that spans the generations, but bear in mind that your youngster may not want a dolls' house – if it is you who really wants that miniature home, go ahead and enjoy it.

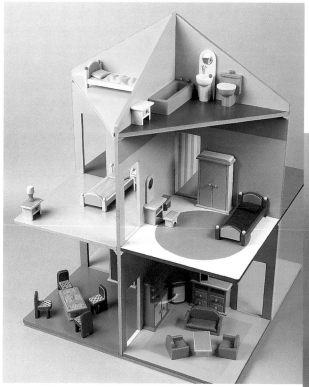

△ ▷ This dolls' house was made for several children to play with at one time. Because there are no exterior walls it is easy for young arms to position their furniture and miniature family with ease.

Inspiration

There are endless ways of decorating a dolls' house and, unless you have a particular passion for one particular style, it is worth considering all the options. The main periods catered for among dolls' house retailers are Tudor, Georgian, Victorian and Modern, but you will also find Regency, Art Nouveau, Art Deco and post-war.

If you are new to the hobby, look through as many books on period interiors as you can – full size, as well as miniature – to help you decide what you like and dislike. If you want to recreate a full-size period home as accurately as possible, it is useful to visit the many historic houses that are open to the public. Take photographs of house exteriors or sketch details that appeal. Look at the furniture styles, the wallpaper and fabric designs, the colours, the paintings on display, the ornaments and the ceramics. Buy a guidebook and postcards to remind you of the interior and help you to build up a portfolio of ideas. File everything under period or type of room – preferably in a scrapbook, or record file with plastic sleeves – and then look for the miniature equivalents.

Videos of costume dramas are also a good source of inspiration. They are accurate in detail as well as enjoyable to watch, and many a television adaptation of a novel or play has found its way into a dolls' house.

When recreating a house, photographs and personal recollections are essential, and the resulting dolls' house will be all the more poignant for the inclusion of items that bring back memories. Local history societies or the Local Records Office may be able to help with your research.

△ Get inspiration from books about different periods.

▷ Antique dolls' houses can inspire. This modern dolls' house kit has been deliberately decorated in the style of an antique dolls' house, and the exterior 'aged' with a wash of grubby paint. Ordinary wallpaper has been used inside, the carpets made from fabric stiffened with iron-on backing, and the balcony is made from kitchen-shelf trim.

Extending the dolls' house

If you already have a dolls' house, consider extending it. The majority of dolls' houses are designed to rest up against a wall. They have plain backs (and often sides) with no windows or decorative features. If you have the space you can utilize this conventional façade to gain access to additional rooms.

The easiest options are to add a conservatory, or whole new wing to either side of the building, or to add a basement beneath. Space permitting, you could add another dolls' house back-to-back with the first. I adapted my Victorian-style dolls' house in this fashion and you could adapt a commercial kit with care. Ideally you should consider such alterations before undertaking any internal decoration, as it will affect your lighting plans.

Creating a rear aspect to your dolls' house allows you to continue with a chosen period when your existing dolls' house is 'full'. But proceed with care when you are adapting a completed dolls' house, and empty it of any furniture and accessories first. The extension should not be permanently fixed to the main house, but held with hook and eye, to retain accessibility to any original lighting scheme.

When butting up a whole new dolls' house against an existing one you need to take account of any roof overhang, and trim it if required to ensure a close alignment. If you use two identical houses, the floor levels and internal wall arrangements will be the same. If you use two different makes of dolls' house do measure carefully when cutting extra doorways

▽ The extended rear of my Victorian dolls' house was made on a separate baseboard. New doorways were cut through from the original house to access the new rooms.

to give access from one house to the other. The new doorways should be precisely aligned.

If you don't want to cut additional holes in your dolls' house use false doors instead, to suggest access from the original house into the new wing. Even without another building, your imagination can provide a whole suite of new rooms behind these false doors, without the bother of having to create them for real. False (or trompe l'oeil) windows can also be used to improve an otherwise blank façade. If you place your enlarged dolls' house on a table with casters, you will be able to reach all sides of the building.

You may not wish to accommodate a whole new house, but perhaps just a conservatory and a garden and, with so many garden accessories available, you will be spoilt for choice. You may need to disguise any existing lighting wires at the back of your dolls' house – perhaps with a strategically placed climbing plant, dovecote, or drainpipe. Looking through from the front of the dolls' house and out through a conservatory helps convey realism.

Windows provide the opportunity to have a balcony – and one at the back of the dolls' house overlooking a garden will add further interest.

△ Theatre or advertising posters can also add interest to an otherwise plain brick wall.

Depending upon the position of your fireplaces you could also position new windows in the sides of your dolls' house, allowing more natural light to enter your miniature rooms.

Other possibilities

You don't have to have a garden at the back of the dolls' house. You could create a mews or garage, or a studio for a craftsman such as a potter or painter. You could have a stable, or perhaps your dolls' house could be the living accommodation for a cattery or a dog's home. You may even want to have a shop or warehouse. Look through books and take notes when out and about for ideas.

Inside the dolls' house

Decorating rooms in your dolls' house is where the fun really starts. There are so many period styles to choose from and this chapter illustrates some of them. Once you are sure where your lighting fixtures are going, you can decorate the walls, ceiling and floor of your dolls' house. Paint charts showing historical colours from DIY stores will help you to select the right colours and, just as with a real house, you can always redecorate when you fancy a change.

Swedish bedroom

Red and white gingham fabric has been used to create this dolls' house bedroom, which is inspired by Swedish furniture and accessories.

Striped fabric was initially inspired by the bunting hung out to celebrate Napoleon's victories and fabrics with a geometric design became increasingly popular in the early nineteenth century and took the form of trelliswork, chevrons and checks, as well as stripes. Regency stripes have long been a favourite for textiles and upholstery.

Imported Indian gingham, a lightweight fabric brightly coloured using vegetable dyes, was typical of these printed checks. The popularity of gingham has endured and it is now available in a number of colours, including yellow, blue, pink and green.

Gingham wallpaper

You will need:
- Gingham fabric
- Scanner or photocopier
- Wallpaper paste

The size of the squares on the gingham check fabric is an important consideration when working in 1:12 scale, so look for the smallest squares possible. To create the gingham wallpaper, either scan an ironed piece of fabric on your computer, or colour photocopy a section as many times as needed. It helps to wrap the fabric over a piece of white mountboard, and to tape it down on the reverse to keep the fabric taut while copying.

Cut into sections and apply to your dolls' house wall with wallpaper paste, as with regular dolls' house wallpaper.

Bed with gingham head- and footboards

You will need:
- A ready-made bed
- Mountboard
- Gingham fabric
- Thin wadding
- PVA glue

1 First, make templates for the bed ends by pushing pieces of paper against the framework of the headboard and footboard to create imprints of the sizes needed. Transfer these rectangular shapes to the mountboard, and cut out two card shapes for the back and two for the front.
2 Cover the front headboard in a thin piece of wadding, to create a 'padded' look.
3 Cut rectangles of gingham ¼in (6mm) larger all round than the four mountboard pieces.
4 Wrap these around the mountboard pieces securing at the back with glue.
5 Leave to dry before gluing one to either side of each bed end, gingham side outwards.

◁ Glue the covered pieces of card to each end of your bed.

Duvet and pillowcase

You will need:

- Gingham and white cotton fabric
- Wadding
- Sewing thread
- Toy stuffing
- Gingham ribbon (optional)

1 Measure your bed and decide what size your duvet will be. Cut two pieces of fabric, one from the gingham and one from the white cotton, adding an extra ¼in (6mm) allowance on all sides for seams. Cut a piece of wadding a little smaller than the intended size of your duvet.

2 Place the wadding on the wrong side of the gingham fabric. With the right sides together sew around three sides of the fabric, occasionally catching in the wadding with your stitches.

3 Turn the duvet the right side out and sew up the remaining side.

4 To make a coordinating pillowcase, sew strips of gingham (or strips of gingham ribbon) across a rectangle of white cotton fabric and use this to make one side of your pillowcase.

Decorative mosquito net

You will need:
- Inner ring from small reel of transparent adhesive tape
- Gingham fabric
- Bridal tulle
- PVA glue
- Narrow ribbon

The inner cardboard ring from a used reel of transparent adhesive tape is ideal for the curtain hoop – simply cut it in half and glue a piece of gingham fabric around it, carefully turning the edges over to the inside, to make a neat finish. Gather two identical lengths of bridal tulle to make the mosquito net, each length should reach from the hoop to the floor. Glue to the inside of the cardboard ring and secure the tulle in place with a bulldog clip while the glue dries. Tie the net back with matching ribbon.

△ Choose a rubber stamp motif to suit your scheme and use this to decorate the wall. Practise on scrap paper first, and position carefully to ensure the stamp is the right way up and equally spaced.

Dressing table

You will need:
- Obeche sheeting
- Ice-lolly sticks
- 4 staircase spindles
- Wood glue

1 Cut the top and sides from obeche sheeting as indicated in the diagram.
2 Cut four staircase spindles to 2¼in (57mm) lengths.
3 Cut two iced-lolly sticks to length to form the long sidepieces. Drill a small hole as indicated to take the towel rail.
4 Glue the pieces together as indicated making sure the curved sidepieces are at the same end of the table.
5 When dry, paint or stain as preferred. Varnish if you wish.
6 To complete, add a rectangle of towelling.

For a country bedroom, use gingham and a plain fabric to make a patchwork quilt. Using large squares of fabric will make the job easier. Alternatively sew strips of gingham ribbon across a plain fabric, or you could use a selection of gingham for an 'American country' effect.

▽ Create matching furniture from cheap whitewood sets.

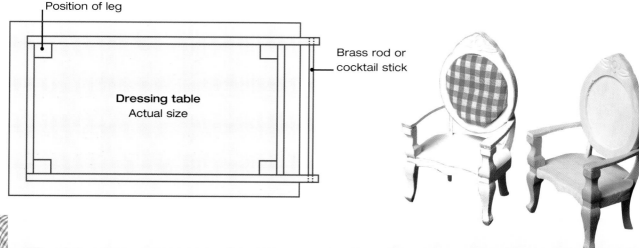

Position of leg

Dressing table
Actual size

Brass rod or cocktail stick

Claude Monet (1840–1926) was one of a group of French artists known as the Impressionists. He moved to his home in Giverny with his second wife Alice, and it was there that he created his now-famous garden. Monet's yellow dining room at Giverny is renowned for its striking colour scheme, which was chosen to display his collection of Japanese prints.

In its purest form, yellow was unknown before the manufacture of chrome yellow, at the beginning of the nineteenth century. Until then ochre pigment was used to create the colour. The arrival of chrome yellow coincided with the neoclassical taste for brilliant colour.

French dining room

This room is inspired by Monet's dining room. Use emulsion paint (sample pots are ideal) for the walls, or use a sheet of coloured paper from an art shop as I have done here.

Terracotta floor tiling

You will need:

- Mountboard in two colours
- Sharp scalpel or craft knife
- Cutting mat
- Metal ruler
- Pencil and set square
- PVA glue

1 Measure the floor space that you want to tile. You will need half of this area in each colour of mounting board, but you should allow a little extra.

2 Each tile will be 1in (25mm) square. Mark out your floor area into a grid, using the set square to provide guidelines for gluing the tiles in place. You may find it easier to fix the tiles onto a piece of card, equal in size to your floor space, so that you can work free of the restrictions of the walls and ceilings.

3 Mark the back of the mounting board sheets into 1in (25mm) squares and cut them out using the scalpel and metal ruler to ensure clean straight edges.

4 Start gluing the squares from the centre of the room. This way any slight fitting discrepancies will work to the edges. Remember to alternate the colours.

Ladder-back chairs

You will need:

- ⅛in (3mm) stripwood
- ³⁄₁₆in (5mm) obeche sheeting
- Mitre block and saw
- Wood glue
- Greaseproof paper
- Fine sandpaper
- Clamp
- Acrylic paint

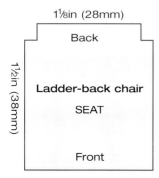

1⅛in (28mm)

Back

1½in (38mm)

Ladder-back chair

SEAT

Front

1 From the ⅛in (3mm) stripwood you need two uprights 3¼in (82mm) long, two front legs 1⅜in (35mm) long, and eight pieces 1⅛in (28mm) long. Cut the seat from obeche as in the diagram.

2 If you want to stain the chairs, do so before gluing, so that the glue doesn't mask the stain.

3 Cut out the various sections and lightly sand the cut edges.

4 Make up the ladder back first, by gluing the shorter lengths between the uprights. Glue the front legs and the crossbar, then leave to dry on a piece of greaseproof paper.

5 When firm enough, carefully remove the back from the paper, slicing with a scalpel if necessary.

6 With the chair back on your work surface, try the seat for a snug fit;

▷ Allow the glue time to dry fully at each stage of this project.

sand if necessary, then glue the seat in place.

7 Carefully glue the remaining front legs and sidebars into position. You may need to hold the chair while the glue begins to take hold.

8 Once the glue is completely dry, paint the chairs with acrylic paint.

Dining table

You will need:

- ⅛in (3mm) obeche sheeting
- ¹⁄₁₆ x ⅜in (2 x 10mm) woodstrip
- Four staircase spindles
- Wood glue
- Sandpaper
- Varnish

1 Cut the table top 4 x 3in (102 x 76mm) from the obeche sheeting. Carefully sand the cut edges, rounding them to a gentle slope.

2 Glue the woodstrip to the underside of the table as in the diagram.

3 Cut the spindles to form the legs to 2¼in (57mm) lengths. Glue the legs in place and when assembly is dry, paint yellow.

4 Varnish the table and chairs when the paint has dried. For a country effect, you could paint, stencil, or stamp a floral design on the chair seats prior to varnishing.

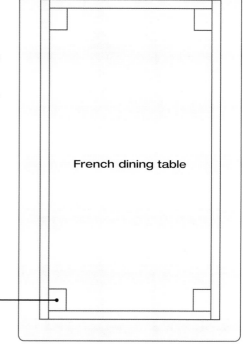

French dining table

Position of leg

Japanese print

You will need:

- Japanese postage stamp or picture from a magazine
- Thin card
- PVA glue
- Picture-frame moulding
- Black acrylic paint

1 Glue the Japanese stamp to thin card, cut a fraction larger than the stamp itself.
2 Cover up any franking marks with a paint colour to match the background.
3 Add picture-frame moulding as with the mirror (see steps 3–4, right), and paint it black before gluing it in place.

Blue and white plates

You will need:

- Miniature paper plates
- Blue and white paint
- A fine paintbrush
- Varnish compatible with the paint

1 Build up a complicated design in several stages. Use two shades of blue paint but add varying degrees of white to alter the colours.
2 First paint the outer rim of the plate, then add the central circle before the finer details.
3 Check that your varnish is compatible with your paint choice to avoid the colour running.

▽ Paper plates are cheap to buy and easy to paint. Look for a design that you can copy from a full-size plate

Mirror

You will need:

- Sheet of mirror card
- Scalpel or craft knife
- Metal ruler
- Cutting mat
- Picture-frame moulding
- Glue
- Acrylic paint
- Masking tape

1 On the reverse of the mirror card mark out a rectangle to the size required.
2 Cut out the rectangle, using a scalpel and metal ruler on a cutting mat.
3 Cut picture-frame moulding to edge the mirror. Mitre the edges, but do not join the pieces.
4 Paint the moulding pieces before gluing them, separately, in position on the mirror card.
5 On the reverse, tape over the area where moulding meets the card, to finish the back.

Lemons

You will need:

- Yellow, white and green polymer clay
- Fine sandpaper
- Cocktail stick

1 Lemons are easy to make. Take a piece of yellow polymer clay about the size of a real lemon pip and blend a small piece of white to one end. Roll into a lemon shape.
2 Add a tiny piece of green, less than a pinhead in size, to one end.
3 Indent this end with the cocktail stick.
4 Lightly roll the lemon over the sandpaper to stipple the skin.
5 Bake according to the manufacturer's instructions.

Floral morning room

This room-box makes a beautiful alternative to a shop interior. Scented
paper is lovely to work with, and it makes the workroom smell delightful
while you complete the project.

The 'forget-me-not' wallpaper used for this room
is a scented drawer liner – the strong design of
the paper provides an interesting alternative to
regular dolls' house designs. When selecting
alternative wallpaper, pay attention to the scale of
any images and avoid large designs, which would
spoil the miniature illusion.

You could take an element of the paper design and
copy it using paint, or cut and paste a small motif
from the paper. Paint it onto other pieces of
furniture using acrylic paint. I have added it to the
backs of the wooden chairs. I also used sections of
the wallpaper on the white wire shelves to create a
coordinated effect.

Varying the internal layout

One of the problems with a room box is that it can look more like a box than a room, but it is easy to improve the room's character with some simple additions. Add a false hall and door to give the illusion of rooms beyond and avoid that 'nowhere to go' feeling sometimes associated with room boxes. Put the hallway section on a platform of MDF and add a short length of balustrade to create two distinct but united areas within the room.

Flooring

Two separate areas of flooring have been created. The raised MDF section is painted white and scored to resemble floorboards. The other area has been 'carpeted' using a piece of upholstery material. This was first backed with iron-on interfacing, cut to size with liquid fabric sealant applied to each edge. The existing selvage edge was positioned at the front of the room.

Day bed

You will need:
- Block of balsa wood
- Plastic railings
- Superglue
- Foam
- Scented drawer-liner paper
- White spray paint

The day bed is made from a block of balsa wood covered with mounting board and scented paper glued around it neatly, like wrapping a parcel. The dimensions were cut to suit the section of plastic fencing used for the back and sides. Remember when cutting the balsa to make allowances for the card. Plastic railings are easy to cut and paint a different colour – in this case, white – and can be secured in place against the base with Superglue.

Sandwiches

You will need:

- Scraps of mountboard
- PVA glue
- Green tissue paper
- Scalpel

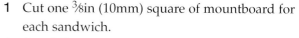

1 Cut one ⅜in (10mm) square of mountboard for each sandwich.

2 Carefully cut each square diagonally in half with the scalpel.

3 Using the scalpel carefully slice off one of the paper sides off each triangular shape of mountboard to leave a rough 'bread-like' texture. If you're using coloured board, it makes sense to peel away the coloured side.

4 Glue the two triangles together with a scrap of tissue paper in between them (to resemble lettuce), making sure that the 'bread' sides are on the outside.

Skirted table

You will need:

- Section of foam pipe insulation
- Cotton fabric (plain or patterned)
- Thin card
- Pins
- PVA glue
- Lace or braid
- Clear acetate sheet

1 Cut a section of pipe insulation 2¼in (57mm) long.

2 Cover each end with a circle of card.

3 Cut a circle of fabric with a 7in (178mm) diameter. Use liquid fabric sealant on the edge or turn a narrow hem. Decorate above the hem of the circle of cloth with lace or braid.

4 Place the cloth right side downwards and put the section of pipe insulation in the middle.

5 Raise pieces of the hem of the cloth to the 'top' of the pipe insulation, securing the fabric at 12 equally spaced points around the bottom edge of the pipe section. Thinking of the base as a clock dial helps. Bring the fabric up against the pipe and push a pin through.

6 Once pinned, turn the table the right way up and add a circle of patterned paper, then a circle of clear acetate, to the top.

Victorian cottage kitchen

Creating a basic room box is easy enough, particularly if you ask your timber merchant to cut the wood for you. The larger the room box, the more space there is for furniture and accessories.

A divided room box is more interesting than a single room, visually as well as creatively. Here a small scullery has been created next to the main kitchen area. Equipping both is easy with the wide variety of accessories available from dolls' house shops, fairs or by mail order.

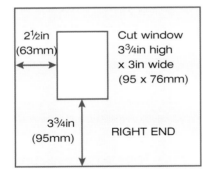

2½in (63mm)

Cut window 3¾in high x 3in wide (95 x 76mm)

3¾in (95mm)

RIGHT END

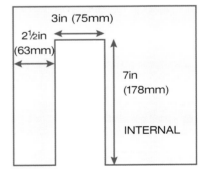

3in (75mm)

2½in (63mm)

7in (178mm)

INTERNAL

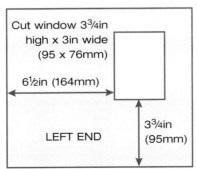

Cut window 3¾in high x 3in wide (95 x 76mm)

6½in (164mm)

3¾in (95mm)

LEFT END

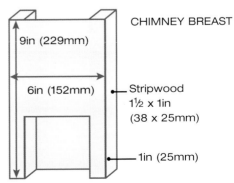

CHIMNEY BREAST

9in (229mm)

6in (152mm)

Stripwood 1½ x 1in (38 x 25mm)

1in (25mm)

The basic room box

You will need:

From ¼in (6mm) MDF cut:
- Base section, 22 x 12in (559 x 305mm)
- Ceiling section, 22 x 12in (559 x 305mm)
- 3 wall sections, each 11¾ x 9in (298 x 229mm)
- Back section, 22 x 9in (559 x 229in)

From ⅛in (3mm) plywood cut:
- Chimney breast front, 9 x 6in (229 x 152mm)

From stripwood cut:
- 2 x 8in (203mm) lengths, for ceiling beams
- 2 lengths of 13¼in (336mm), for ceiling beams
- 2 lengths 1½ x 1 x 9in (38 x 25 x 229mm), to support chimney breast
- Several lengths to make the false back door

- Oak for beams (optional)
- Textured white paint
- Sample pot of black masonry paint
- Wood glue

1 Cut out the room pieces as indicated. The ceiling beams are optional but they add character. In this project lengths of real oak have been used. The internal wall needs to be notched at intervals to take the beams if you decide to feature them.

2 Cut the apertures for the windows and internal door as determined by the fixtures that you are installing. Here, the windows have been positioned 3¾in (95mm) up from the floor and the door is 7 x 3in (178 x 76mm).

3 It is easier to paint the walls before assembly and textured white paint, as used here, is effective. Stain the oak beams to suit; here, very dilute black paint has been smudged on, to suggest an aged appearance.

4 Glue the pieces together. The back wall rests on the base, and the three walls butt up against the base and back wall. You may decide to keep the roof free, so that it can be removed to help position accessories.

5 Position the chimney breast wherever you wish on the back wall, and secure with wood glue when you are happy with its placement.

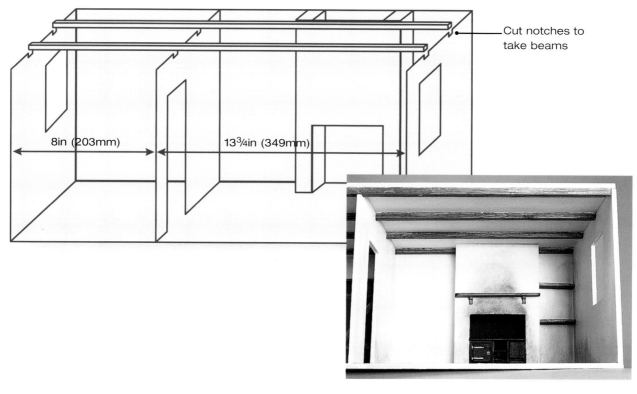

8in (203mm) 13¾in (349mm)

Cut notches to take beams

Flooring

I used two sheets of resin flooring which can be bought in a 'red tile' and 'flagstone' effect. Making a paper pattern of the floor is advisable to get a good fit. The resin sheet is easy to cut with household scissors and can be secured in place with PVA glue. Apply the glue lightly to the surface, cover with a piece of thin card and smooth over to enable even pressure to be applied to the sheet surface.

Doors

Doors can be bought. Here each door has been made from obeche sheeting scored to resemble planks, and then stained. A doorframe has been made from leftover moulding from other projects. You can buy a variety of catches and handles from dolls' house shops or by mail order. The internal door has been glued so that it is partly open.

Accessories

The wash copper is faced with more resin paper, this time in a brick-effect. The chimney flue is made with a piece of mountboard cut to size and scored to fold.

The chairs and table were made following the instructions given in the French Dining Room project (see page 22) and oak wood stain was applied with a paintbrush. Remember to stain the wood first, as it doesn't adhere to glue and can leave pale patches.

Tables are easy to make using ⅛in (3mm) wood sheeting and staircase balusters for legs. I added an open false drawer to give the impression of the kitchen in use. Kitchens are always a hive of activity, so add plenty of accessories and 'work in progress' for that lived-in-look.

Variations

The room box with its dividing wall can become any manner of room combinations and you can use carpeting and wallpaper for a totally different effect. Try these examples for yourself.

Bedroom with en suite bathroom
Shop with stockroom
Bedroom and nursery
Living room with kitchen
Parlour with study
Café with kitchen
Photography studio with darkroom
Surgery and waiting room
Gallery with office

Edwardian gentleman's study

William Morris wallpaper and sombre colours have been used to create
a room with a distinctly masculine feel for the Edwardian era.

Raising the floor

Part of the floor has been duplicated and raised on scrap wood to add interest to a basically square room. Both sections of the floor have floorboards, made from ⅜in (10mm approx.) strips of wafer-thin wood laid in lengths, and stained with an oak wood-stain. The raised library section is edged with a section of staircase components.

On the desk

Glue a rectangle of thin leather to a cheap bought desk, and paint bands of black and gold paint around the top. Pile the desk high with papers, maps, books and accessories. Papers can be 'aged' with a wash of cold tea or coffee and left to dry.

The blotter is a rectangle of card cornered with green leather. The ink well is a bead with a trimmed feather as a quill. Add a piece of paper to a bought typewriter for authenticity – simply fold it around a short length of black dowel and glue to the top.

Collector's cabinet

△ The display area is lined with a piece of red dolls' house carpet and tiny rock and gem-stone samples have been glued onto it.

You will need:
- Bought chest of drawers, or bottom half of a dresser
- Scraps of stripwood
- Wood stain
- Wood glue
- Tiny fragments of gemstones (from museum or gift shops)
- Matchsticks
- Clear acetate for lid

1 Use stripwood to make a top frame to sit on top of the chest of drawers. The back should be higher than the front.
2 Stain the pieces before gluing them together.
3 Cut a piece of dolls' house carpeting to fit inside.
4 Edge the inside with matchsticks, to hold an acetate lid in place.
5 Replace original handles with more fanciful versions of your choice.
6 Glue small pieces of rock and gemstones in the cabinet or make polymer clay birds' eggs.

Studies are popular rooms to create for the dolls' house. A study can incorporate a library to give that learned, bookish feel, or be more relaxed, like a studio.

Storage chests

You will need:
- Woodstrip
- Wood stain
- Cardboard box
- Cotton crochet thread

To make a large travelling storage box, stain or paint some woodstrip, then glue lengths of it over a small cardboard box. Make a lid, and hinge this to the box using a length of fabric tape glued under the top back strip.

   Make two holes a short distance apart in the two side panels. Thread a length of cotton crochet thread through them to make carrying handles, and your crate is complete.

▽ You can make any size crate that you need. Save wood shavings for packing material.

Wing armchair

You will need:

- Balsa wood, ¼in and 1in (6mm and 25mm) thickness
- Balsa cement
- PVA glue
- Leather
- Brass pins
- Sandpaper

1 Cut out the pattern pieces in balsa wood, as shown in the diagrams.
2 Smooth the sides with sandpaper.
3 Glue together using balsa cement. Make sure that the seat back is between the two sides.
4 Glue the base piece between the sides and base and leave to dry.
5 When dry, cover the chair with leather. Use the chair pattern as a guide, but cut the leather a little larger all round, so that it will turn over the edges of the chair.
6 Start with the outside of the sides and pull the leather taut as you glue. Snip around the curves and glue the overlap to the inside of the chair.
7 When the sides are done, cut a length of leather the width of the seat, to cover from the base over the seat and up over the back. Glue and pull taut just over the top of the chair back.
8 Cut a final piece of leather to cover the back and base of the chair. Leave to dry. Glue four beads to the base and add brass pins to represent studs. Add a cushion if wished.

Wing armchair
To scale

SIDES
Cut 2 in ¼in (6mm) thick balsa

BASE
Cut from 1in (25mm) balsa

BACK
¼in (6mm) thick balsa

Butterfly specimen case

You will need:

- Images of butterflies
- Thin card
- Matchsticks
- PVA glue
- Clear acetate

1 Cut a piece of card 1 x 1¼in (25 x 32mm).
2 Carefully cut out several images of butterflies.
3 Mount each butterfly on a tiny piece of card to raise it from the background.
4 Glue the butterflies to the card.
5 Edge the card with painted matchsticks cut to length.
6 Glue a piece of acetate on top and paint the edges black to provide a border.

△ Colour photocopy suitable images and reduce in size if necessary. The pictures of butterflies shown here were found on the back of a greetings card.

Antique books

Real miniature books, with readable text, blank pages or dummy books can be bought but, if you want to fill your shelves with 'antique' spines, you can make your own dummy versions by gluing pictures to blocks of balsa wood.

Look for pictures of rows of book spines in magazines and catalogues, and scan on your computer or colour photocopy to 1:12 scale (or to fit you shelves). Cut a block of balsa wood to fill the shelf recess and glue a length of book spines to one long edge. Use the back of a scalpel blade to carefully define between each book, and then paint the top of the block.

Separate a run of these dummy books with the odd individual volume that can be withdrawn, and insert the occasional bundle of papers to create realism.

▽ Runs of dummy books are quick and easy to make, and you can rapidly fill up whole bookshelves.

Cut a piece from a cork tile to make a pin board. Curl the edges of pinned notes by running them over the blade of scissors.

Look for suitable images to mount on cardboard and frame them with miniature picture moulding.

Use a metal thimble as a waste paper bin.

Cut the head off a plastic toy tiger and make a flat body out of felt; paint on acrylic stripes.

The globe-shaped pencil sharpener was a lucky find in a gift shop.

▽ Wrap a length of embroidery canvas around a make-up bottle or film canister to make the umbrella stand and glue a strip of leather around the top to finish it off. The butterfly net is made from a loop of wire with a net bag sewn to it attached to a bamboo skewer handle.

The living room

Dolls' house enthusiasts are often concerned about creating interiors that are historically accurate, but it can be liberating to go against the grain and allow your imagination to fly. Here are three different scenarios to illustrate how you could decorate a modern living room.

Fun colours

We've all seen those television programmes where designers choose alarming shades of magenta or turquoise and create a 'retro-chic with hint of neo-classical boudoir' effect. With fun in mind this room experiments with colour. A mobile phone-holder in the shape of a translucent yellow plastic chair and a sheet of wrapping paper provided the starting point for this room setting.

This is an opportunity to use one of those vibrant matchpot colours that you wouldn't dare paint on the walls at home, but would secretly like to try. Look in 'pound shops' or gift shops or even

look at pet accessories for brightly coloured or gimmicky objects that could fit in with your crazy scheme.

The plastic chairs were given foam cushions courtesy of a jewellery gift box. The wooden furniture was painted in colours picked from the wrapping paper that was used instead of conventional miniature wallpaper – but take care when using wrapping paper, as it can be quite thin, so you need to spread your glue or paste carefully. The flowers in the vase were punched out of craft foam sheeting and threaded onto beading wire.

▷ A retro room that is decorated just for fun. Forget all those historical references and put in what you would like to see there. Magazines can provide lots of ideas.

Picture books

▷ All coffee tables should have suitable books. Books with coloured pictures are easy to make and suitable images can often be found in interiors magazines.

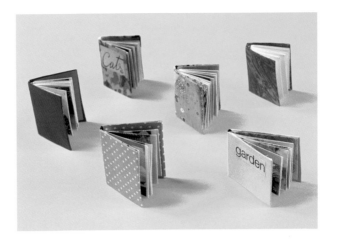

You will need:
- Magazines, catalogues, tourist brochures
- Plain A4 paper
- Patterned paper for the cover
- PVA glue
- Lightweight cardboard

1. Turn a sheet of A4 paper to 'landscape' shape, and divide it into vertical strips that are $\frac{7}{8}$in (22mm) wide.
2. Rule a margin about $\frac{1}{2}$in (13mm) from the left-hand side, and then rule 14 lines from left to right each $\frac{3}{4}$in (19mm) apart. There should be another margin remaining at the right-hand side of the page. Each horizontal line will be one book and each divided space will form a page of the book.
3. Cut a template to the size of a page and use this to cut out images from magazines, perhaps selecting a particular topic for each book.
4. Glue the images to each page, leaving the margins clear. Look for a printed word to stick on the first page of your book.
5. Either cut out each strip, or colour photocopy the page.
6. Using a metal ruler, cutting mat and scalpel cut between each horizontal strip of pictures.

7. Fold up each strip between the pictures, like a concertina. Fold the margins too.
8. Apply glue sparingly to the reverse of each strip and fold up again, pressing each fold carefully to form the pages of the book.
9. At the spine of the book glue a rectangle of plain paper to hold together the paper fold. Leave to dry.
10. Cut a piece of cardboard a little larger than the opened-out book. Score two lines vertically the width, and position of, the spine. Glue the book spine into the cardboard one.
11. Cut a piece of patterned paper a little larger than the cardboard cover and glue it to the book, notching the corners neatly. Fold the paper around to the inside of the covers.
12. Finally, cut and glue further pieces of paper over each of the inside covers, to make a neat finish.

◁ Modern, even minimalist interiors should make the most of the variety of textures available.

Adding texture

This 'textured' room is in direct contrast to the funky colours of the previous scheme. I've tried to incorporate a variety of tactile surface materials, while keeping to a neutral colour scheme to emphasize the variety of textures involved.

Textured wallpaper is available at any DIY store, but look for smaller-scale designs. Here two designs are used – a basket-weave pattern and a vertical line, united by colour. Hessian material provides the flooring but it must be glued carefully as excess glue seeps through the threads. The floor was livened up with a fur-fabric rug, though the pile has been trimmed in an attempt to keep it in scale.

A walk along the beach provided sea-worn driftwood to create the mirror frame, much as in a real room. A shell has been used as an ornament on the shelves joining the 'ivory' bead vase, gem stone, stone Buddha, and metal picture frame. Chunky pieces of balsa wood have been glued together to make the basis for the leather sofa and clear plastic mapping pins make perfect furniture feet. The side table is a gift box and holds the glass and decanter. A small strip of copper foil adds a contrast to the wood logs in the fireplace. The finished room wouldn't look out of place in a modern interior magazine!

Fusion

Fusion is a concept as old as time rather than a modern idea, but it has satisfactory 'designer speak' overtones. It is simply the mixing of the old with the new and, in the dolls' house, it enables you to have rooms with a mixture of period and modern miniatures.

Most of us are already experts at fusion in our real homes, as we combine inherited 'hand-me-downs' with our own latest purchases. Transferring this concept to the dolls' house is the easiest option of all. However, while combining the old and the new is a natural progression in this hobby, there are several ways to avoid the 'jumble sale' effect.

- Stick to one particular colour scheme whether it is a single colour or a limited range. You can combine furniture from different periods but be choosy about the wood. A contrast between light and dark wood is possible, alternatively select just one wood, all pine, oak or mahogany.

- Be selective about the different patterns that you have in wallpaper and fabrics. Plain colours work well with traditional patterns. Try combining floral wallpaper with plain upholstered seating. If one pattern dominates keep all other surfaces plain.

- Don't be tempted to fit everything into one room – try to be selective working on the 'less is more' principle. Include some glass in the room scheme – a vase of flowers works wonders thanks to its translucent nature.

- A simple blind at the window provides essential dressing, without competing for attention with the other elements of the room. The same goes for the floor. A plain floor-covering acts as a foil to busy walls.

Dolls' house gardens

Dolls' house gardens are enjoyable to create. They are usually made as a separate unit to butt up against the dolls' house, but some commercially available dolls' houses now include a small area of external space to turn into a garden. With the variety of accessories and miniature plants available, interpreting the outdoor room is as variable as dealing with an interior.

Greenhouse

Giant mushrooms grow where plant food has spilt over the window sill onto the neighbouring grass. Inside a parrot, two lizards and even a snake enjoy the burgeoning jungle of their neglected greenhouse home.

Rather than buying a 1:12 scale greenhouse, I adapted a plastic container that was designed to house cacti. Although it resembles a miniature room, it is not scaled for the dolls' house and it falls short at its front elevation to be realistically 1:12 scale. To solve this problem, I raised its overall height with lengths of stripwood and replaced the original base with a piece of MDF cut over-size. This extra outside space can be used for additional accessories such as a watering can, animals, wheelbarrow, water butt, dog kennel, or even 'wild' flowers.

This greenhouse is designed to be freestanding but, to give the illusion of an entrance, I glued a fake door to the back wall, having replaced the original 'glass' wall with MDF. I then added a horizontal row of bamboo skewers to support climbing plants at the top of the conservatory.

Drilling a series of holes into the front and back walls and cutting the skewers to length is straightforward, but I advise painting the skewers before finally fitting them in place.

▷ A cautious fox runs past the laden wheelbarrow, towards the compost heap.

▽ When you remove the lid you can clearly see the bamboo skewers in place.

Potting bench

To make a potting bench, insert a length of stained timber into the original slot for the floor and support it on timber legs made from square dowel. I used a mini power drill with a cutting blade to create broken panes and the appearance of cracks in the 'glass'. If you want to emulate this, be careful, as the edges of the broken plastic are quite rough.

Planting beds

To make chunky planting beds, use a strip-timber edging and fill them with polystyrene (or florist's oasis). Paint the top layer of the polystyrene brown and glue tea leaves to the surface to represent soil. Make holes and insert your plants.

△ Any commercially available miniature greenhouse can be given the exotic treatment.

Garden planter

You will need:

- Small box, approx. 2½in wide x 2¾in tall x 1in deep (64 x 70 x 25mm)
- PVA glue
- Stapler
- Gummed paper tape
- Oasis
- Brick-texture cladding (or paper)
- Tea leaves
- Selection of foliage

1 Cut the box in half and staple together to form a right angle.
2 To strengthen the box cover the outside with gummed paper strips. To make it even sturdier, you could cut pieces of mountboard to size, and glue them to the inside of the box.
3 Glue texture cladding (or cheaper brick paper) to the outside of the box.
4 Cut a piece of oasis to fit each section of the planter. Spread glue on each top surface and sprinkle with tea leaves to resemble earth.
5 Make holes in the oasis with a skewer and glue in the plants of your choice.

▽ Raised flowerbeds are effective against a dolls' house wall, or freestanding in the miniature garden.

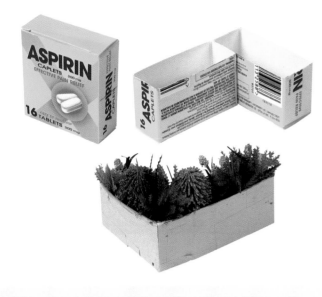

Compost heap

You will need:

From ⅛in (3mm) square stripwood:
- 4 uprights 2½in (64mm) long

From 10 x 2mm stripwood:
- 10 crossbar pieces 1½in (38mm) long

From balsa wood:
- 1 back panel piece 2 x 2¼in (51 x 57mm)

From stripwood:
- 4 front panel pieces 2in (51mm) long

- Wood glue
- Polystyrene
- Brown paint
- PVA glue
- Tea leaves and snippets of floral material

A compost heap is easy to make and can be put anywhere in your dolls' house garden.

1 Glue five of the crossbars between two of the uprights like a ladder, starting at the bottom and leaving very small gaps in between to make one side panel. Repeat to make the other side.
2 Glue the two upright sections to the back panel.
3 Glue the four pieces of stripwood across the front of the compost heap, making sure that there is a gap at the bottom for the 'compost' to spill out.
4 Cut a piece of polystyrene to the size of the compost heap, paint it brown on all sides, and fit it in place between the sides and back. Glue some tea leaves and snippets of floral material to the top surface with PVA glue.
5 Glue tea leaves around the bottom to represent the fully composted material spilling out.

Miniature plants

Realistic miniature plants can be purchased, but you might prefer to use or adapt fake fish-tank plants and plastic or silk flowers to fill in between your more choice specimens. You can also make your own foliage from scratch, using wire, paper, polymer clay and other bits and pieces.

▷ Exotic red flowers bloom inside the greenhouse. These were made from polymer clay, shaped onto thick twigs, and painted with acrylic before varnishing.

◁ Fill up a wheelbarrow with spare flower pots.

Dog kennel

Why not make your miniature dog his own special house in the garden?

You will need:

- Clapboard wood panels (or mountboard)
- Mountboard
- Sandpaper
- ⅛in (3mm) square stripwood
- PVA glue
- Wood glue
- Acrylic paint in green and brown
- Small hook

1 Cut the two sides, back and front out of the clapboard wood panels.
2 Cut the base from mountboard.
3 Use wood glue to fix lengths of stripwood along the inside edge of both sidepieces.
4 Glue the four sides and the base together.
5 Cut a piece of mountboard large enough to cover the top of the kennel and form a pitched roof when folded in half. Cover this with a piece of sandpaper and paint it green.
6 Paint the outside of the kennel brown.
7 Screw in a small hook to hold the dog's lead to the side of the entrance.

△ Make room in your back yard for a kennel.

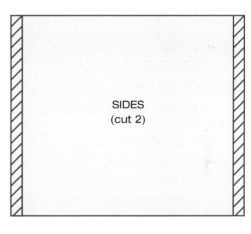

SIDES
(cut 2)

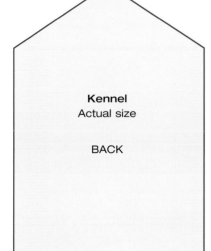

Kennel
Actual size

BACK

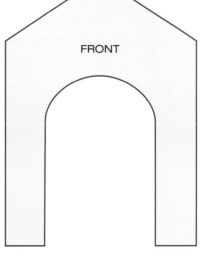

FRONT

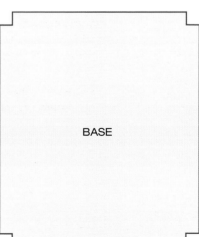

BASE

Cottage garden

This scene was inspired by a real cottage garden. I have used a little artistic licence in my miniature interpretation, although I have tried to include some recognizable plants, such as the hollyhocks (from a kit) and the foxgloves

The garden is constructed on a 12in (305mm) 'corner' of ¼in (6mm) MDF, made from a base and two sidepieces glued together with wood glue. The back wall has been cut 2in (50mm) shorter to allow a trellis section to be added. The back wall is covered with sections of wood cladding and the other walls are covered with inexpensive brick paper.

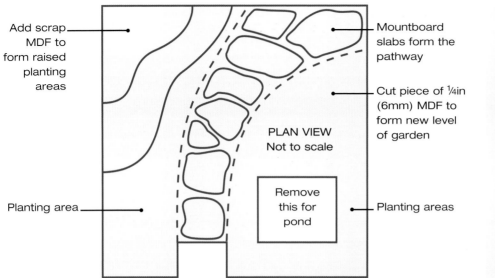

Add scrap MDF to form raised planting areas

Mountboard slabs form the pathway

Cut piece of ¼in (6mm) MDF to form new level of garden

PLAN VIEW
Not to scale

Planting area

Remove this for pond

Planting areas

Tip
To make cladding look more weathered, carefully slice sections with a sharp craft knife, and sand slightly before staining with wood dye. Colour in some of the individual bricks on commercial brick-effect paper to vary their uniform tone.

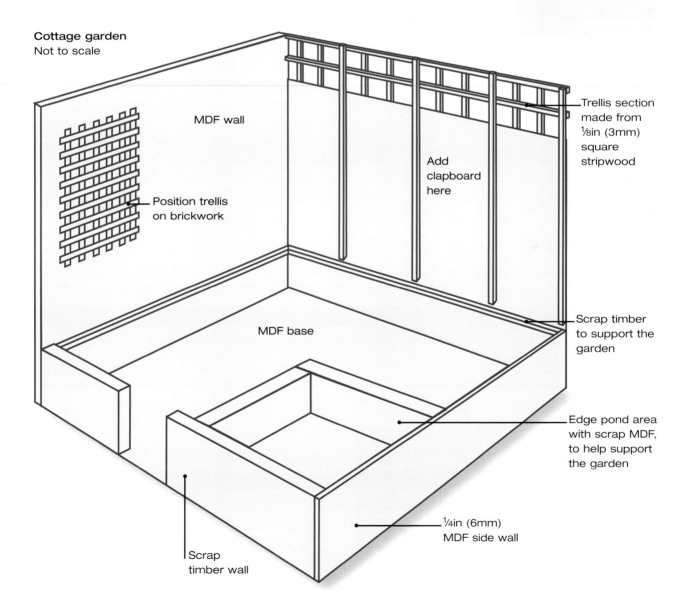

Cottage garden
Not to scale

MDF wall

Add clapboard here

Trellis section made from ⅛in (3mm) square stripwood

Position trellis on brickwork

MDF base

Scrap timber to support the garden

Edge pond area with scrap MDF, to help support the garden

Scrap timber wall

¼in (6mm) MDF side wall

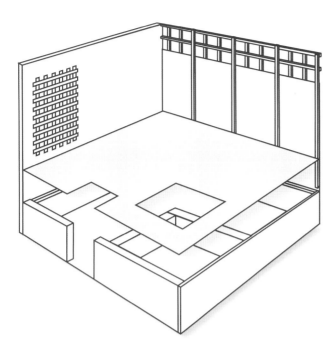

△ In order to create the pond, I raised the main level of the garden using ¼in (6mm) MDF supported on scrap timber, and allowed a 2½in (64mm) inlet for the steps. Do not glue this in place until the pond surface has been made. Further scraps of wood have been added on top of this section to create the raised flowerbeds.

The pond

You will need:

- Two pieces of clear acetate 4 x 2in (102 x 51mm)
- PVA glue
- Lichen
- Small stones
- Balsa wood
- Black acrylic paint
- 1:12 scale terracotta tiles
- Foliage materials

1 Edge the inner sides of the 4 x 2in (102 x 51mm) pond recess with balsa wood painted black.
2 Glue small stones and foliage material to the base of the pond.
3 Sandwich some lichen between the two sheets of acetate with a little glue and press a heavy weight on top while the glue dries.
4 Glue the acetate beneath the open hole of the pond to create the illusion of the water's surface.
5 Edge the pond with terracotta tiles, allowing for a slight overhang.
6 Glue more foliage material around the tiles to soften their edges.

The plants

The hollyhocks, clematis and morning glory are all made from commercially available kits. There are several suppliers of realistic miniature flowers, but it is possible to make your own from a variety of sources.

The delphiniums and orange poppy-flower heads are all made from discs of tissue paper cut using a hole punch. These have been pushed in

their centres with a rounded stick into a soft surface (a computer mouse mat is ideal) to shape them. Create stems from thin wire wrapped in florist's tape, and glue the flower heads appropriately into place with PVA.

The foxglove flower heads have been made from a thin strip of tissue paper rolled up into a tube shape. You may have to hold each flower while the glue sets when gluing to a wire stem.

Liberal use has been made of foliage – available for the model railway – the smallest from a range of conifer trees makes its appearance at the rear of the garden.

The path is made from irregular-shaped pieces of mountboard, covered with multi-purpose filler, and painted once this had dried. It is edged with wooden shingles, cut shorter and painted to resemble terracotta.

Japanese garden

It is possible to buy a number of Japanese miniatures to use in a garden such as this one and garden centres can be a useful source for tiny pagodas as well as gravel and stones.

The simplicity of Japanese gardens makes them easy to recreate in miniature, in contrast to the English country garden. Admittedly mine is a little more complicated, due to the inclusion of a koi pool, but in terms of planting it is easy. The main structure is a rectangular box with a raised area for the home, and the pond is created from a cut-away section of MDF.

Cactus dressing, seeds, or lentils can be used to represent the traditional gravel. Spread the area you wish to cover with a thick layer of PVA glue then scatter on the seeds. Leave to dry before carefully tipping to remove the excess. Balsa wood can be shaped into rounded stones and positioned into groups or alone. Spray with a textured paint to add realism. Use green railway scatter material around the bases and rounded bushes from railway model shops as shrubs.

Pond

When incorporating the pond, first make large stones from balsa wood, sliced off near the top. Glue them either side of your acetate 'water' to give above and underwater sections.

Screening panels

To make screening panels, cut bamboo skewers to size and glue them onto pieces of cloth to hold them together. Paint in suitable colours using acrylic.

Shoes

The Japanese leave their shoes at the door. The chunky shoes are easy to make from balsa wood.

You will need:
- 2 blocks of balsa, each ¾in long by ⅜in wide by 5⁄16in thick (19 x 10 x 8mm)
- Black and coloured acrylic paint
- Varnish
- Thin leather for straps

1 Remove a piece from one end of the balsa to create a wedge shape, and sand gently to curve the toe and heel.
2 Paint the sole in black acrylic. Paint the sides in a bright colour and the top in yellow, with thin stripes across in a basket-weave pattern. Add tiny dots or flowers to the sides when the initial coat of paint is dry. Varnish the sides when the paint is dry.
3 Make three holes in the top for the shoes straps, one at the front and two either side of the heel.
4 Use a thin leather thong to make a 'Y' shape, wrapping a short piece over a longer one. Glue the ends of the 'Y' and push them into the holes. Leave to dry.

△ Little shoes are easy and fun to make. Add to your costume hire shop if you don't have a Japanese dolls' house.

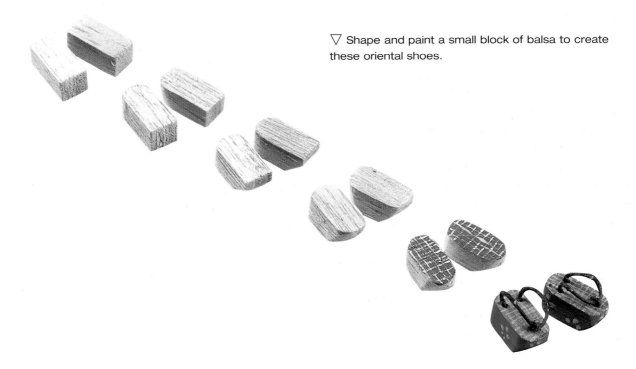

▽ Shape and paint a small block of balsa to create these oriental shoes.

Creating shops

There are many styles of dolls' house shops on the market, but here I show you how to make a 'halfway house' and suggest some ideas for decorating the exterior, as well as for making produce to sell. The ideas can easily be transferred to a conventional miniature shop.

Basic shop

The halfway house can be made from one sheet of 4 x 2ft
(1220 x 610mm) MDF, which is cheap to buy from a DIY shop or timber
merchant.

The basic plan uses ready-made windows and doors. The precise size of the base is variable, depending upon how much street space you want to take your own accessories, such as street furniture, a bicycle, café tables, or a seat. You can also bring the scene to life with pedestrians, discarded wrappings, and a dog and cat.

To make the basic shop

You will need:

- 4 x 2ft (1220 x 610mm) sheet of MDF
- Jigsaw
- T-square
- Sandpaper
- Wood glue
- Panel pins
- Hammer
- Router (optional)
- Safety glasses
- Protective mask
- Masking tape
- Wood filler

1 Mark out the MDF as shown on the cutting plan and construct the house using simple butt joints. If you have a router, make slots in the side sections to receive the floors, adding twice the routing depth to the width of the floors before cutting out.

2 Cut out each section using the jigsaw. Wear safety glasses and a protective mask because of the dust particles.

3 Plane, rout, or sand the top of the house front to an angle of 45°, so that the roof section will fit comfortably in place.

4 Make paper templates of the windows and doors and use these templates to determine where the windows and doors should be positioned. Space

Basic shop cutting plan

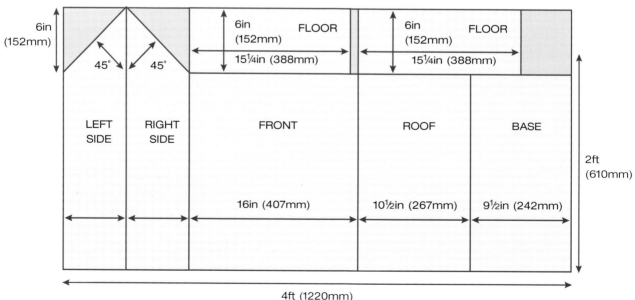

the windows equally, if possible, and bear in mind that the first floor will be 8½in (226mm) up from the base. Use a drill to make the initial holes for the windows and doors, then the jigsaw to cut out the shape. Don't worry if your saw-line is not completely straight, as most doors and windows come with frames that overlap the cut edge.

5 Sand down each hole to eliminate small bumps and nicks.

6 Hold the sections together with masking tape to check the fit.

7 Pencil in a line 8½in (226mm) from the base then, with the house on its back, use wood glue to fix the floors to the sides along this pencil line. If necessary, use masking tape to hold in place until the glue dries.

8 With the house still on its back, glue the front panel in position. When dry, glue the main structure to the base, using panel pins to help secure it.

9 Add cornices to give additional support to the floors, cutting and mitring them as appropriate. Use wood filler to disguise any cracks.

10 Glue and pin the roof section, then the building is ready for decoration.

Basic display units

All shops need to display their goods, and basic units can be made from mountboard or ¹⁄₁₆in (2mm) thick wood. Mountboard is easiest to cut – using a metal ruler, sharp scalpel and a cutting mat – and it bonds well with PVA. Mountboard is easily coloured with acrylic paint and, once varnished, the units are ready to be filled.

Variations

There are many ways of altering a dolls' house to make it unique. These include:

Adapting an existing dolls' house by inserting additional bought windows in one of the sides, or in a dormer in the roof (the size of the required aperture should be on the window packaging).

Adding a porch, window boxes, wooden shutters, a front step, railings or drainpipes. Look at real houses for guidance.

Adding a chimney by cutting a short stack out of wood or card.

Bakery/café

Install a café above your shop, instead of domestic accommodation.
Making bread and cakes is great fun and easy to do. Remember that
your establishment could also make use of a delivery boy and bicycle,
paper bags and cake boxes.

Open-backed counter

You will need:

Mountboard cut in the following pieces:

- Top: 4 x 1in (102 x 25mm)
- Sides: cut 2 from 3 x 2in (76 x 51mm) card, shaped as in diagram
- Front lower panel: 4 x 1in (102 x 25mm)
- Back lower panel: $3\frac{7}{8}$ x 1in (98 x 25mm)
- Bottom shelf: $3\frac{7}{8}$ x $2\frac{1}{8}$in (98 x 54mm)
- Middle shelf: $3\frac{7}{8}$ x $1\frac{7}{16}$in (98 x 37mm)

- PVA glue
- Acrylic paint

1 Paint all the mountboard pieces – making sure the paint isn't too watery, or it will warp the card. Glue the pieces together once the paint is dry.
2 Start by gluing the back panel between the sides.
3 Glue the front panel in place, in front of – and flush with – the sides and the bottom edge.
4 Next, glue the bottom shelf in place, then the top one.
5 Use narrow offcuts of card to create shelf supports; glue these to the sides and then glue the middle shelf in position.
6 Varnish when dry.

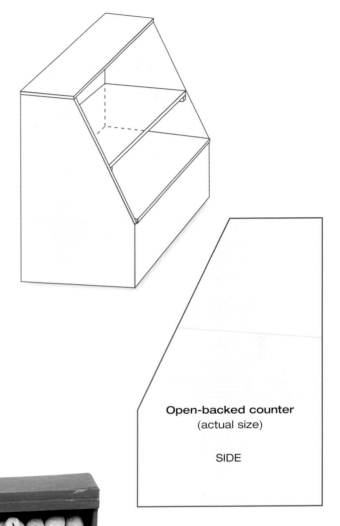

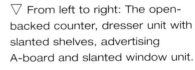

Open-backed counter
(actual size)

SIDE

▽ From left to right: The open-backed counter, dresser unit with slanted shelves, advertising A-board and slanted window unit.

Dresser unit with slanted shelves

Make the base cupboard and top separately, then glue them together.

To make the base cupboard

You will need:
Cut from mountboard:
- Back panel: 3 x 4⁷/₈in (76 x 124mm)
- 2 sides: 3 x 1¹/₂in (76 x 38mm)
- Top panel: 5¹/₈ x 1³/₄in (130 x 44mm)
- Skirting panel: 4⁷/₈ x ¹/₂in (124 x 13mm)
- Lower shelf: 4³/₄ x 1⁹/₁₆in (120 x 39mm)
- Middle shelf: 4³/₄ x 1¹/₂in (120 x 38mm)
- Supports: ¹/₂in and ¹/₈in (13mm and 3mm) strips

- PVA glue
- Acrylic paint

1 Glue the sides to the back panel.
2 Glue the front skirting panel to the sides.
3 Glue the lower shelf in place on top of the supports.
4 Paint and varnish the assembly, the middle shelf and top panel, and leave to dry before proceeding.
5 Glue the middle shelf in position.
6 Glue the top shelf in place, flush to the back, leaving an equal overhang at both sides.

Dresser unit base cupboard
(Not to scale)

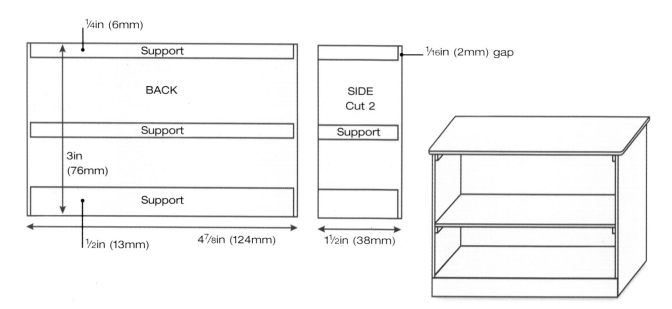

To make the top unit with slanted shelves

You will need:

Cut from mountboard:
- Back panel: 4⅞ x 3¾in (124 x 95mm)
- 2 sides: 3¾ x 1in (95 x 25mm)
- Top panel: 4⅞ x 1¹⁄₁₆in (124 x 27mm)
- 2 shelves: 4¾ x 1¹⁄₁₆in (120 x 27mm)
- Top front fascia: 4⅞ x ½in (124 x 13mm)
- 3 front strips: 4⅞ x ¼in (124 x 6mm)
- Shelf supports as in diagram

- PVA glue
- Acrylic paint

1 Glue supports in place on back and side panels.
2 Place the back piece on your work surface and glue the sides to the back.
3 Glue the top in place.
4 Paint the assembly and the shelves.
5 Apply glue sparingly to back and sides of shelves and slide into position.
6 Glue the top front fascia across the top, and fix flush with the top panel.
7 Glue one of the front strips to the top front fascia, and the other two across the shelf fronts.
8 Touch up any unpainted areas. Varnish when dry.

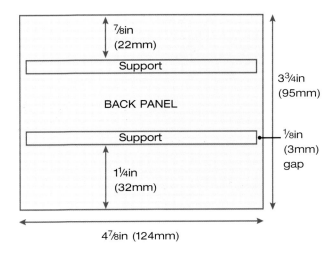

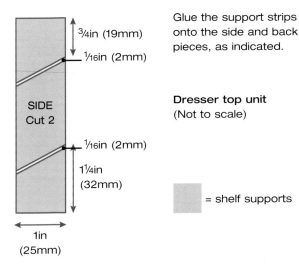

Glue the support strips onto the side and back pieces, as indicated.

Dresser top unit
(Not to scale)

= shelf supports

Advertising A-board

You will need:

- 2 rectangles of mountboard, 1¾ x 2¼in (44 x 57mm)
- 4 lengths of ⅛in (3mm) square wood, 3¼in (82mm) long
- Small strips of leather
- 2½in (64mm) piece of thread
- PVA glue
- Acrylic paint

1 Paint the card black on both sides.
2 Paint or stain the square wood uprights. Glue the uprights together at the top, using the leather strips.
3 Make a hole in the lower edge of each panel, thread through the string and tie to secure.

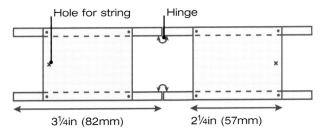

Hole for string   Hinge

3¼in (82mm)   2¼in (57mm)

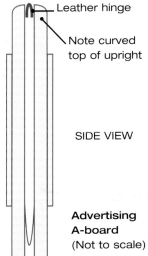

Leather hinge

Note curved top of upright

SIDE VIEW

Advertising A-board
(Not to scale)

Slanted window unit

The height of the front panel should be equal to the distance from the shop floor to the bottom windowsill. The back panel needs to be ¼in (6mm) more than this, so adjust the plans as required.

Slanted window unit
Not to scale

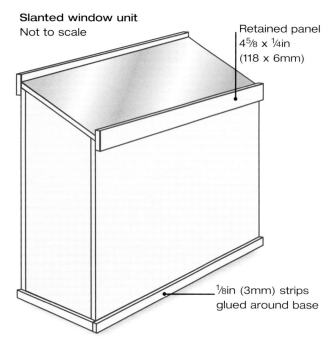

Retained panel
4⅝ x ¼in
(118 x 6mm)

⅛in (3mm) strips
glued around base

You will need:

Cut from mountboard:
- Front panel: 2¼ x 4⅝in (57 x 118mm)
- Back panel: 4⅝ x 2¾in (118 x 70mm)
- Two sides: 2¾ x 2¼ x 1in (70 x 57 x 25mm)
- Top: 4⅝ x 1³⁄₁₆in (118 x 30mm)
- Two fascia panels: 4⅝ x ¼in (118 x 6mm)
- Offcut strips: ⅛in (3mm) wide

- PVA glue
- Acrylic paint

1 Glue the sides between the front and back panels and allow to dry.
2 Glue the top in place.
3 Glue the two fascia panels in place, one at the front and one at the back, so that they to stand proud of the top by ⅛in (3mm).
4 Glue the ⅛in (3mm) strips around the base of the unit, to trim.
5 Paint, and varnish when dry.

Bread and biscuits

Air-drying clay is perfect for making bread products. Keep surplus clay covered when it is not in use as it dries out quickly. Keep a dish of water nearby and use it to clean your fingers and to smooth over any cracks in your loaves.

You will need:
- Air-drying clay
- Water
- Acrylic paints in browns, yellows and ochres
- Varnish
- Ornate buttons (optional)

Make a batch of bread, so you have enough for your bakery, the dolls' house kitchen and the delivery boy's basket.

To make a loaf, take a small piece of clay and shape it as desired – cottage, French stick, sandwich or bloomer. If the clay appears to crack, smooth it over with a little water. Clean your hands often to avoid particles of clay drying on them. Put the loaves to one side to dry, preferably overnight.

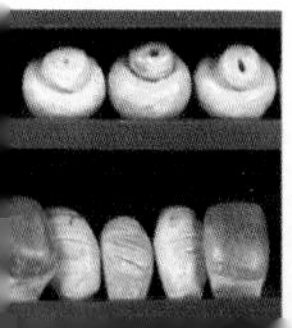

When the bread is thoroughly dry, you can paint it. Dab a selection of suitable colours on a palette and use these for each loaf over a basic

yellow or brown base coat. Paint and re-paint as necessary, until you are satisfied with the results, but bear in mind that the colours will look very flat until you apply a coat of varnish.

To make a basic biscuit, squash a small ball of clay and, if cracks appear at the edges, smooth them with the water. Leave the biscuit to dry, then paint: black dots can resemble currants, and red dots, cherries. Varnish and, when dry, glue piles of biscuits onto plates or trays.

Cakes can be made in a similar fashion. Look for buttons with a swirl pattern: these can be

squashed into the top of a cake shape to resemble a cream topping.

Toffee apples can be made from coloured beads glued onto short lengths of cocktail sticks, which have been trimmed with a scalpel to make them thinner. Glue the toffee apples to a plate, to keep upright.

Make skirted tables following the instructions for those in the Floral Morning Room on page 26, and a menu stand by pushing a brass pin through a butterfly earring back and gluing on a piece of paper for the menu.

Confectioners

It is fun filling a sweet shop with confectionery. There are some wonderful miniature products that you can buy but, if you prefer to make your own confectionery, I suggest some ideas below.

The façade has been divided into two by a length of fancy moulding. Brick-effect paper has been aged with a little acrylic paint above, and with stippled plaster below. A large picture window has been cut, acetate inserted, and a simple stripwood frame added. Rubdown transfer letters were used for the name on the windowpane.

Tip
Before committing the letters to their final position on the window, draw up a pattern and lay the window over it to check that the letters are straight, evenly spaced, and in the correct position. Do this before inserting the window in place.

Panelled base unit

You will need:

Cut from mountboard:

- Back panel: 3¾ x 2½in (95 x 64mm)
- Front panel: 3¾ x 2½in (95 x 64mm)
- 2 sides, each: 2½ x 1in (64 x 25mm)
- Top: 3¾ x 1⅛in (95 x 28mm)
- 3 decorative panels, each: 2 x 1in (51 x 25mm)
- Offcut strips: ⅛in (3mm) wide

- PVA glue
- Acrylic paint

1 Glue the sides between the front and back panels.
2 Glue the top in position.
3 Edge with the ⅛in (3mm) strip around the top and base.
4 Glue the three decorative panels to the front.
5 Paint, and varnish when dry.

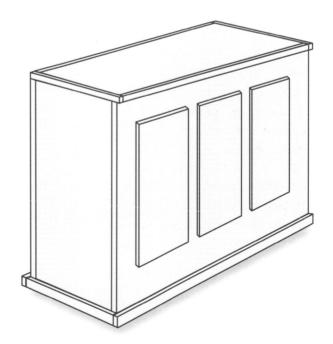

▽ From left to right: panelled base unit, dresser with straight shelves, dressing table (see page 20) used as a counter, and slanted window unit.

Dresser unit with straight shelves

Make this unit in two parts, and then glue them together. The base is made in exactly the same way as the dresser in the baker's shop on page 56.

For the top unit
You will need:

Cut from mountboard:

- Back: 4³⁄₄ x 3³⁄₄in (120 x 95mm)
- 2 sides: 3³⁄₄ x 1in (95 x 25mm)
- Top: 1¹⁄₁₆ x 4³⁄₄in (27 x 120mm)
- 2 shelves: 4⁹⁄₁₆ x 1in (115 x 25mm)
- Strips for shelf supports: ¹⁄₄in (6mm)

- Scalloped-edged paper
- PVA glue
- Acrylic paint

1 Lay the back on the work surface and glue the two side panels in place.
2 Glue the top panel in position across the top. Glue the shelf supports to the inside back and sides at required heights. Paint in your choice of colour.
3 While the assembly is drying, paint the shelves.
4 Apply glue sparingly to back and sides of shelves and secure in position. Varnish when dry.
5 Cut narrow strips of scalloped-edged paper (folding concertina fashion makes this easy) and carefully decorate the shaped edge with pinpricks. Glue to the shelf edges.
6 Glue this top unit to the base cupboard.

Ideas for making sweets

Wrap rectangles of balsa wood in pretty paper and add a ribbon and a paper label to make boxes of chocolates for display.

Cut sections of wooden dowel and wrap in paper to represent tins of sweets.

Craft foam makes excellent 'sweet' material: part-cut rectangles of brown craft foam to represent bars of fudge and toffee.

Pink and white craft foam stuck together and cut into bars makes excellent coconut ice.

Carefully cut plastic tubing into sections to make sweet jars. Add a cardboard base and a lid. Fill with tiny squares of craft foam or beads to represent sweets.

Look for colourful, suitably shaped buttons and beads to stick on cardboard or metal trays.

Cut small 'bars' from cardboard and wrap in gold or silver foil. Wrap a slightly narrower band of paper around the middle and add detail with a gold pen. Glue the bars into a display box, leaving some loose for cutomers to pick up.

Display boxes

You will need:
Thin card
PVA glue
Acrylic paint

1 Trace the templates onto thin card.
2 Cut out carefully and score along the fold lines.
3 Fold the tabs behind the head and end pieces, glue into position and leave to dry.
4 Paint in a colour of your choice. Add a name or logo in gold.

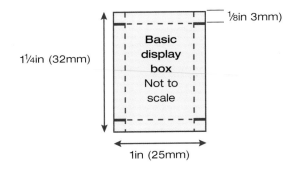

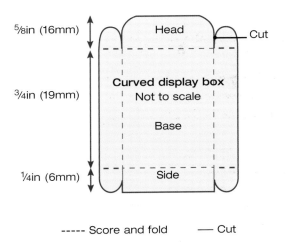

----- Score and fold   —— Cut

Toy shop

This toy shop has a large bay window on the ground floor, and a small dormer window in the roof. I've added winter snow (made from washing powder) to give a seasonal touch and to evoke the excitement of Christmas.

If using a bay window for your shop, removing the glazing bars will make the goods inside more easily visible. Create a base for the bay window to stand on, made from sections of balsa wood cut to shape. Balsa wood is easy to sand but does create an irritating dust, so it is advisable to wear a dust mask.

Use mountboard to create a counter that fits into the bay from the inside of the shop.

Wall-hung tiles

The tiles on the upper front of the toyshop are made from ¾in (19mm) wide strips of textured paper bought from an art shop. Carefully shape each tile on the strip and highlight some of the tiles with brown acrylic, to vary the colour and produce a more realistic effect. Solid blocks of colour never look authentic, as buildings are not uniformly clean.

Roof tiles

The roof tiles are cut from strips of deep red mountboard ⅞in (22mm) wide. Make cuts along the strip ⅞in (22mm) apart, but do not cut right through to the top. Glue a thin strip of mountboard along the lower edge of the roof and then glue the first strip of tiles onto this to allow a small overhang. Overlap the next strip remembering to stagger the cuts. When all the strips are glued in place give the roof a wash of brown acrylic paint.

The interior

The attic of the toyshop has been trimmed with woodstrip to represent beams and the floorboards on the first floor have been cut from strips of balsa wood stained with wood dye; commercial tiled flooring – covered with clear sticky-backed plastic to make it shiny – has been used in the shop. Remember that any of the toys made for the shop can also be used in the dolls' house nursery.

Hobby horse

Drill a small hole in the base of a chess-piece knight (cut it from base if necessary). Insert a length of bamboo skewer. Paint as desired, then add an embroidery thread bridle.

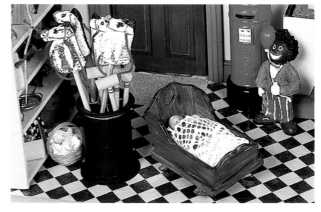

Toy castle

You will need:

- Mountboard
- Yellow and black acrylic paint
- ⅛in (3mm) stripwood
- Black net
- Needle and thread
- PVA glue
- Balsa wood
- Green scatter material

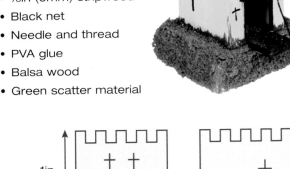

1in (25mm)

1⅛in (28mm)

1 Cut out four pattern pieces from the mountboard and cut an entrance in one piece. Paint on both sides, adding slit windows.

2 Glue the four pieces together and strengthen with stripwood, glued around the inside like a battlement.

3 Make holes for the drawbridge and 'thread' in the castle walls and the drawbridge (made from a scrap of card) itself. Take the thread from underneath the drawbridge, through the castle wall, along the top of the doorway, back through the castle wall and down to the drawbridge again, knotting underneath to secure.

4 Stick black netting behind the open door to represent the portcullis.

5 Glue the castle onto a balsa wood base to make the hill. Spread with glue, and cover with green scatter material. Alternatively, glue to a square of mountboard.

Sledge

Cut lengths of ice-lolly sticks to form a wide 'ladder' for the top of the sledge and glue two more pieces for the runners. Paint as desired, and add a string handle.

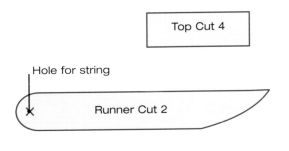

Top Cut 4

Hole for string

Runner Cut 2

Sledge
To scale

Greengrocer

Greengrocer shops are fun to make, because of the opportunity
to make a wide and colourful range of fruit and vegetables. Polymer clay
is best for this purpose, and you don't need to be that talented to come
up with credible results.

When using brick-effect paper, apply it carefully over the whole front and sides. Do not cut out the windows and door until the paper has completely dried, and then do so cleanly with a sharp scalpel. Colour some of the individual bricks with a little acrylic paint, so that they don't look too uniform.

No 'glass' has been used in the shop window – the area has been left open to show off the fruit and vegetables to greater effect. A length of brass rod has been inserted across the window area, to provide a hanging area for bananas.

Display counter

Create two angled display counters from mountboard or wood, one for inside the shop window, and the other for outside. The sizes depend upon the height and width of your window. The depth of the internal counter in this case is 2¼in (57mm), with a 1¼in (32mm) difference in height between the front and back to create the slope. Cover the slope with a rectangle of sheet-grass material (from model railway shop), allowing a slight overhang on all sides.

Outside the window the angle of the counter isn't as steep, with just a ⅜in (10mm) difference in height. The front counter has been made from mountboard faced with wood cladding in sheet form, but you could recreate this effect by scoring lines with a scalpel against a metal ruler. Make small paper bags out of a large one and secure together with cotton.

Storage

Use stripwood to create boxes for your fresh produce. These boxes are 1½in (38mm) by 1¼in (32mm). Add shortened matchstick lengths into each corner. Leave some boxes empty and stack them up inside the shop.

Make sacks from a rectangle of coarse weave material, 3 x 4in (76 x 102mm). Fold in half, sew along the bottom and up the open side. Turn through and part-fill with grains of rice before gathering the top closed.

Apron

Cut out the apron from the fabric of your choice (cotton is best) and apply liquid fabric sealant to the edges. Cut a length of fabric or ribbon for the neck and glue into place. Tie the apron on your doll.

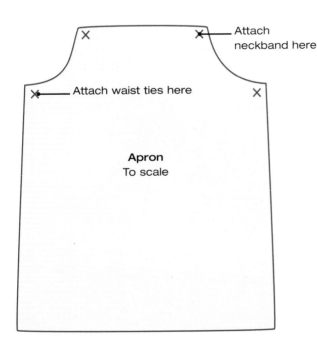

Apron
To scale

Attach neckband here

Attach waist ties here

Fruit and vegetables

You will need:
- Polymer clay in a variety of colours
- White tile or smooth surface
- Cocktail stick
- Fine sandpaper
- Scalpel
- Tile or clean baking tray for oven

Making fruit and vegetables from polymer clay is easy, but make sure you keep your hands clean throughout the making process to avoid colour contamination and follow the manufacturer's instructions for baking your finished produce.

Tomatoes
Roll red clay into small balls. Indent one end slightly with the cocktail stick and add a tiny piece of green clay to the indented end.

Oranges
Roll balls of orange clay and indent one end slightly with the cocktail stick. Gently roll each orange over a piece of fine sandpaper to texture the skin. Add a tiny piece of green clay to the indented end.

Pears
Take small pieces of green and yellow clay, blend together and form into a pear shape. Indent the top end. Roll out a thin stalk of brown clay and push this carefully into the indent. Cut a small leaf shape from green clay and add to some of your pears.

Cauliflower
Make the cauliflower floret from cream clay, or blend white with a touch of yellow. Make pinpricks all over the floret, then make each leaf separately as follows:

Take a small ball of dark green clay and roll it into a flat circle – or squash it from finger to finger – to make it very thin. Wrap this shape around the floret, making sure that the base is covered. Add more leaves to build up the cauliflower, then curl the top edge of some of the leaves over the cocktail stick to shape.

A cabbage or lettuce can be made in the same way by using green leaves over a green centre.

Carrots
Roll a piece of orange clay into a cone shape. Very carefully roll the scalpel over the top of the carrot to create lines, but not cuts. After baking, rub a little brown paint over the carrots to highlight these marks. Add a touch of green clay, green paint, or reindeer moss to the top, to resemble the leaves.

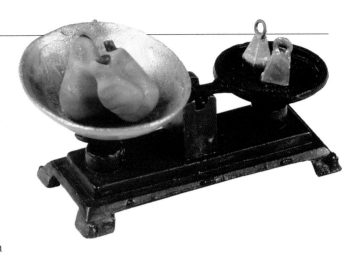

Onions

Blend orange and brown clay together to create a suitable colour. Wrap onion layers around a central core in a similar fashion to the cauliflower. Use the scalpel to make tiny vertical lines on the skin.

Peas

Make a batch of pea-green clay by blending green and yellow. Reserve a little of this and make a lighter green. Shape tiny pieces into a curved moon shape to make the pods. Select some of the pods and slit open with the scalpel. Widen out the pods with the point of the scalpel and insert tiny balls of the light green clay. Stick a number of the pea pods together before baking, for ease of transference.

Parsnips

Make in the same way as the carrots but use cream clay and increase the size slightly. Make lines on the carrots with a scalpel (see 'Carrots') and brown the skin in the same way.

Spring onions

Roll tiny sausages of white clay and slightly longer and broader sausages of green. Fuse the two together with a squeeze and a roll. Flatten the green end and cut (like fingers) to form the leaves. When baked, dip the ends in glue and dip into brown scatter material. Glue a piece of miniature newspaper into the box before putting the spring onions on top.

Leeks

Make like the spring onions but larger. Use stubby lengths of green and a longer piece of white. Use the scalpel to make nicks in the green stem to represent the leaves.

Turnips

Squash a cone-shaped piece of white/cream clay onto a ball of purple. Carefully roll the turnip to firm the shape. Use the scalpel to make markings on the skin, as with the carrots. Add tiny dots of white and two or three strips of green to the purple, to make the leaves.

▽ Make fruit and vegetables for your dolls' house kitchen as well as for the greengrocer's shop.

Antique shop

An antique shop is a useful repository for all the miniatures you have collected or made, but not yet housed. Once you have your dolls' house, simply go shopping in your own miniature store to furnish it.

Rather than keep the smooth surface of the MDF, the front of this antique shop has been given a thin covering of multi-purpose interior filler. This was quickly stippled with a household cleaning sponge to add texture before the plaster set and the surface then painted with cream emulsion paint. If you want to position a sign on your shop front, mask that area first, to keep it clear and smooth. The topiary trees shown here would look equally grand outside a smart town house, or either side of a conservatory door.

Window blind

You will need:
- 2 x 2½in (51 x 64mm) piece of fabric (or to cover window area)
- Liquid fabric sealant
- Thin cord
- Picot braid
- Small bead
- 2in (51mm) length wooden dowel/cocktail stick

Smart window blinds are perfect for this establishment and an easy alternative for those who find bulky curtains a chore.

1 Cut lower edge of fabric into a curve.
2 Apply liquid fabric sealant to all edges.
3 Glue cord to mid-point of lower edge on the reverse side.
4 Glue picot braid along lower edge of reverse and front side.
5 Add parallel length of braid to front.
6 Carefully glue bead to end of cord.
7 Glue the wooden dowel along the top edge of the blind and roll up a short section of the fabric.
8 Glue the blind to the inside of the door.

Model ship

You will need:

- Balsa wood
- Cocktail sticks
- Stiff white fabric
- Cotton thread
- Small brass pins
- Acrylic paint
- Varnish

1 Fashion a hull, approx. $2\frac{1}{8}$ x $\frac{1}{2}$in (54 x 13mm), out of balsa wood. Sand it gently to achieve the required shape, making sure that the base of the boat is flat.

2 Cut three cocktail sticks into $1\frac{5}{8}$in (41mm) lengths, and one $\frac{3}{4}$in (19mm) length.

3 Push the sharp end of the cocktail sticks into the boat to form the masts.

4 Cut three sails from stiff white fabric.

5 Sew the sails to the masts using cotton thread. You will find it easier to anchor the thread with a brass pin carefully pushed into the boat. It doesn't matter if the sewing is a bit rough, as it forms the rigging.

6 Paint and varnish the hull, and mount the boat on a wooden base.

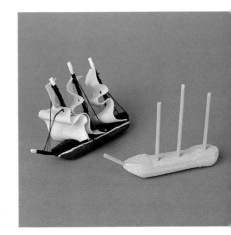

Oriental ornament

Look in charity shops and boot sales for oriental scenes. These are often made from paper and thin cork and found in a glass case, which you will need to remove carefully. The finished display would be suitable for a Victorian study or gentleman's club.

Oriental bird scene

You will need:

- Matchbox
- Thin stripwood or mountboard
- Acrylic paint
- PVA glue
- Piece of acetate or plastic

1 Retain the delicate features of the oriental scene using tweezers.

2 Cut down the tray of the matchbox to the same width as the stripwood.

3 Glue lengths of stripwood to the outside of the matchbox, to strengthen it.

4 Paint a background scene on the inside of the tray, and paint the outside brown.

5 Glue the birds and cork leaves into position at the bottom edge of the tray.

6 Cut a piece of acetate to cover the box, and glue it in place.

7 Paint a thin line around the edge of the acetate, to resemble a wooden frame. Add tiny gold dots for nails at the corners.

Lion-skin rug

You will need:

- Piece of sheepskin
- Polymer clay (or animal head)
- Deep orange beads
- Acrylic paint

1 Cut out the animal shape from the sheepskin.
2 Trim the hair very short, but leave a collar around the neck area to represent the mane of the lion.
3 Apply a wash of dull yellow to parts of the skin, to age it.
4 Either cut the head off a toy lion, or model a lion's head from the clay, using a picture of a real lion as guidance. Make the lower jaw as a separate section and push the beads into the eye sockets.
5 Paint the head once the clay has dried and add a dab of black and white to the eyes.
6 Glue the head to the body, pulling the hair around the neck.

Donald Deskey screen
Half actual size

Cut shapes from silver foil

Donald Deskey Screen

Donald Deskey (1894–1989) collaborated with designer Paul T. Frankle to produce screens and cabinetry in lacquered and metallic leaf finish, with vivid, jazzy decoration featuring zigzags. He was the principal designer for the Radio City Music Hall in New York.

Use black paper and foil to make this striking Art Deco screen

You will need:

- Black mounting board
- Silver foil
- Orange paper
- Black paper
- PVA glue
- Black fabric tape

1 Cut out three rectangles from the black mountboard as in the diagrams. Cut out the silver foil as indicated, remembering that it is the duller side of the foil that will show on the front of the screen.
2 Glue the foil to the correct panel and carefully smooth it with a soft cloth.
3 Cut thin strips of orange paper and glue these in place as indicated.
4 To make the hinges, glue lengths of fabric tape to the back edges of the middle panel, leaving half of the width of the tape exposed.

5 Glue the respective side panels onto the tape, leaving a small fraction of the tape clear to ensure that the tape folds.

6 Cover the back of each panel with a rectangle of black paper cut to size.

Topiary trees

You will need:
- Paper-pulp balls in three sizes
- Bamboo skewer
- Acrylic paint in green and brown
- PVA glue
- Green and brown scatter material
- Oasis

1 Thread the paper balls onto the skewer. Leave large gaps between the balls, make sure that the smallest ball is threaded on last, and that the skewer isn't pushed all the way through it.

2 Paint the paper balls green, and leave to dry.

3 Cover each ball with PVA glue then sprinkle on green scatter material while rotating the skewer to ensure even coverage. Leave to dry.

4 Carefully remove the balls and paint the skewer brown.

5 Thread the balls on the skewer, this time leaving a small gap between each one.

6 Fill a mini plant pot with oasis. Spread the top with PVA glue and sprinkle on brown scatter material. Leave to dry, then tip off the excess.

7 Trim the skewer, then insert into the oasis with a dab of PVA glue.

Clarice Cliff Plates

Clarice Cliff (1899–1972) was influenced by avant-garde Paris, and she produced some of the most striking pottery of her time, designing over 2,000 patterns with names like 'Sunray', 'Solitude', 'Appliqué' and 'Tennis'. Very much a career girl she married her boss, and inspired other women to seek roles other than motherhood.

▽ These charming plates can be completed in several simple stages.

You will need:
- Miniature paper plates
- Acrylic paint in various colours
- Fine paintbrush

1 Paint the outer rim of a plate orange, using a fine paintbrush. Paint another circle inside this one in a yellow-orange colour. Paint 'cloud-like' leaves in orange, darkening the colour towards the outside of the foliage.

2 Add a green mound at the bottom edge of the design. Paint fields in pale green strips and add the trunks of the trees in a very dark blue. Highlight the very edges of the foliage, and add a dark blue outline between the two rim colours.

Country home store

This shop could incorporate a variety of miniatures: garden ornaments and pots, cushions and rugs, bags and baskets, and even 'home-baked' foodstuffs. You may choose to identify it with a particular geographic region or favourite holiday destination.

This country home store uses the basic shop plan shown on page 52, but here the exterior has been given a Tudor look. This has been achieved by using ordinary textured wallpaper available from the DIY store, and stripwood, painted black, for the 'beams'. This façade could also be used for a conventional dolls' house.

Door

This door is made from ⅜in (10mm) thick balsa wood, scored to resemble planks, and stained brown. A section has been cut away, and plastic inserted to make a window. The door has been glued closed, to dispense with small hinges and pins. Sections cut from plastic fencing provide ornate hinges and a front door handle.

Window boxes

These have been made from painted mountboard and filled with a selection of foliage material.

Roof

The roof has been painted with emulsion and acrylic paint, to give the impression of thatch. First paint the roof in two shades of brown, blending the colours to give darker and lighter patches, then use a fine paintbrush to add short strokes of paint in burnt sienna and yellow ochre, working from the lowest edge of the roof to the ridge.

Wallpaper

Before applying the wallpaper, give the MDF a coat of ordinary wallpaper paste. Allow it to dry. Cut the wallpaper to fit the various sections. Paste all the wallpaper to the walls, then paint in cream emulsion and over-paint in white. Vary the thickness of the paint, to allow a little of the cream to show through and give an 'aged' look.

Stripwood

Once the wallpaper is dry, cut stripwood to length. Cut and notch each edge of the stripwood by scraping a scalpel blade along it, away from you, so that the stripwood doesn't look too straight. Measure the corner upright lengths first, and make a pencil note on the dolls' house and on the back of each length of stripwood, to indicate where the pieces will fit once they are painted. Paint the stripwood before gluing into position. How you position the stripwood is up to you – look through books on houses of this period for inspiration.

Hexagonal display plinth

Cut out the unit using the template. Score along each of the vertical lines, enough to fold cleanly but not cut through. Glue at the join with PVA, but secure on the inside with a strip of masking tape. Glue the hexagonal top in place. Once dry, paint in the colour of your choice and, when that is dry, varnish. Make two more hexagonal units.

By using a variety of heights you can glue the hexagonal plinths together in an arrangement to suit your shop display. Top with dolls' house carpet, or with some marble-effect paper for a grander impression.

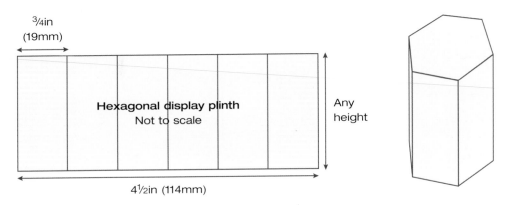

¾in (19mm)

Hexagonal display plinth
Not to scale

Any height

4½in (114mm)

Storage chest

You will need:

Cut from mountboard:

- Base: 3 x 1½in (76 x 38mm)
- 2 ends: 1¼ x 1⅝in (32 x 41mm)
- 2 sides: 3 x 1¼in (76 x 32mm)
- ³⁄₁₆in (4mm) strips

- PVA glue
- Acrylic paint
- Polystyrene (optional)

1 Glue the side panels to the base.
2 Glue the end panels in place against the sides and base.
3 Glue the narrow strips around the base to trim.
4 Paint, and varnish when dry.
5 If wished, fill the bottom of the chest with a rectangle of polystyrene to raise the contents, and make them easier to view.

Stepped display unit

You will need:

Cut from mountboard:
- Base: 4 x 3¹³⁄₁₆in (102 x 96mm)
- Sides: cut according to template
- Top and bottom treads: 1 x 4in (25 x 102mm)
- Middle tread: ¾ x 4in (19 x 102mm)
- Three risers: 1 x 4in (25 x 102mm)

- PVA glue
- Acrylic paint

1 Glue stepped sides to base panel, flush at the back.
2 Glue treads in place on the steps.
3 Glue risers in place starting with the lowest.
4 Paint sides and risers. Varnish when dry.
5 Decorate treads with wallpaper.

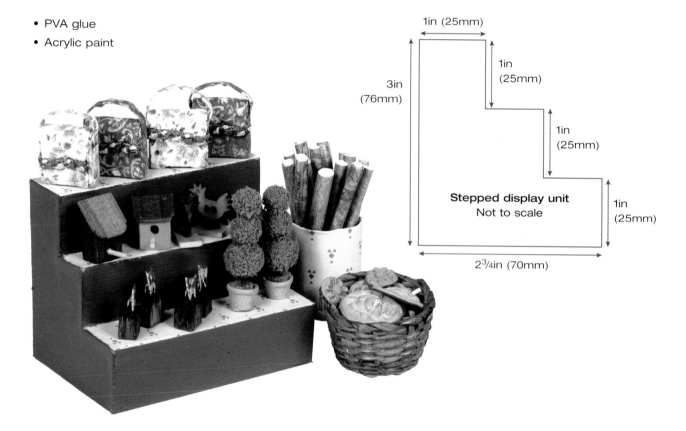

1in (25mm)

1in (25mm)

3in (76mm)

1in (25mm)

Stepped display unit
Not to scale

1in (25mm)

2¾in (70mm)

Lady's bag

You will need:
- Block of wood, 1 x ⅞ x ⁵⁄₁₆in (25 x 22 x 8mm)
- Floral cotton fabric
- Braid
- Brass pins

1 Sand the top of the block into a smooth curve, to make a bag shape.
2 Glue two pieces of fabric to each end of the 'bag', overlapping to the main body.

3 Cut a piece of fabric, 3¼ x 1½in (82 x 38mm). Glue a ⅛in (3mm) hem on the long side.
4 Glue a piece of braid along one of the shorter edges of the fabric, securing the ends to the wrong side of the fabric.
5 Apply glue to the wrong side of the fabric and wrap it around the wood.
6 Make a narrow handle from a 2½in (64mm) strip of fabric. Glue to the bag sides. Hammer a small pin into the handle ends to represent a rivet.

Herb display rack

You will need:

From mountboard:

- 2 sides: 2¾ x 1¼ x 2¹¹⁄₁₆in (70 x 32 x 68mm)
  + slope
- Top: 3 x 1¼in (76 x 32mm)
- Six strips: 3 x ½in (76 x 13mm)

- Matchsticks
- PVA glue
- Acrylic paint

1 Glue top onto the slope of the sidepieces.
2 Glue one strip across the front, and secure to the sides to form a skirting board.
3 Glue another strip at the top slightly proud of the sides to create a lip. Paint the assembly and the remaining strips.
4 Glue the last four strips across the back of the unit, with the bottom one flush with the floor and the top slightly proud.
5 Cut four matchsticks to fit and glue to the top, to create three separate divisions.
6 Paint the matchsticks, and varnish when dry. Fill the completed rack with herb pots.

Shelves

You will need:

Cut from mountboard:

- Back: 3 x 3in (76 x 76mm)
- 3 shelves: 3 x ½in (76 x 13mm)
- 2 sides: 2⅜ x ⁹⁄₁₆in (61 x 14mm)

- PVA glue
- Acrylic paint

1 Curve the top corners of the shelf unit.
2 Paint all the shelf unit pieces.
3 Glue the three shelves to the back.
4 Glue the sides against the outside of the back and shelf ends.
5 Varnish when dry.

Herb pots

Take a small ball of air-drying clay and fashion it into the shape of a simple pot. You can sand the top edges when the pots have dried, so don't worry too much about the bowl rim. When dry, simply glue in foliage material.

The pots have been displayed on a slanted shelf made from mountboard. Cut out the sections as in the diagram, glue, paint and varnish. If you have a large shop you can put two of these display racks back to back.

¼in (6mm)

2¾in
(70mm)

Herb display rack
Not to scale

SIDES
Cut 2

1¼in (32mm)

Terracotta plaques

Brooches, buttons and jewellery can be used to make moulds. Press the shape into a thick pad of polymer clay (any colour), remove the shape and bake the polymer clay according to the manufacturer's instructions. The mould can be used over and over again.

Either use polymer clay or terracotta air-drying clay to recreate the shape. Press the clay into the mould trying to keep the back as thin as possible. Carefully peel away the clay and leave it to dry overnight. Dry-brush a little white acrylic paint onto the plaque, then dab away with a cloth to remove any build-up of paint and to leave a slight highlight. The lion-shape plaque here is ideal as a decorative wall feature or, with the insertion of a small piece of wire flex (electrical wire minus the wire) to resemble a spout, it could be used as a wall fountain.

Bird boxes

Make bird boxes from pieces of scrap wood, ½ x ⅞ x ¾in (13 x 22 x 19mm). Cut the top at an angle and top it with a piece of roof shingle cut to size. Paint the box before adding the roof. Drill two holes, and insert a small piece of cocktail stick into the lower one to form a perch. Paint the top hole black, using the pointed end of a cocktail stick inserted into the hole.

Preparation table

You will need:
- Top: 4⅞ x 1⅝ x ⅛in (124 x 41 x 3mm) wood
- 4 banister spindles cut to 2¼in (57mm)
- 2 stripwood sides: 4⅜in (112mm)
- 2 ends: cut to fit
- Cocktail stick
- Wood glue

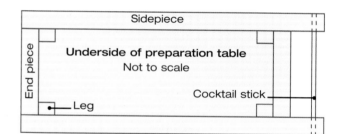

1 Tape the two sides together and sand one end into a curve.
2 Drill a hole through both pieces of the curved end.
3 Paint or stain all wood pieces if wished.
4 Glue the sides to the underneath of the table top, extending over one end.
5 Measure, cut and glue in ends.
6 Glue the legs into position.
7 Insert a cocktail stick through the drilled hole.
8 Glue a strip of brown paper to the cocktail stick and roll it up.
9 Trim the ends of the cocktail stick flush with the sides and gently sand smooth.

Accessories

Glue suitable buttons onto small pieces of wood to make animal sculptures.

Make scatter cushions from 1½in (38mm) squares of fabric. Sew a plain and a patterned square together around three sides, right sides facing. Turn the right side out and fill with rice. Sew up the remaining side.

Look for small earrings with a butterfly wing clip. Reserve the clip for another use. Bend the pin downwards and insert into a small square block of balsa. Stain the balsa and, hey presto, you have an ornament.

Make miniature topiary trees from painted, very small paper-pulp balls; cover them in scatter material, and thread onto short lengths of cocktail stick. Plant into a piece of oasis or air-drying clay in a tiny pot.

Roll up offcuts of wallpaper to make giftwrap and put into a film canister covered in wallpaper.

Flower arrangements

Bought miniature flowers can be mixed with those from other less conventional sources:

- Look in haberdashery departments or craft shops for paper and silk flowers designed for hats and bridal trims. Those with a smaller flower head, or a multitude of small florets, can be taken apart and the individual pieces used in a miniature flower display.

- Bottle tops and metal lids make ideal vases. The metal ones can be squashed into a more pleasing oval shape.

- Plastic bottle tops can be painted or covered with tape to make containers. Fill with a selection of foliage and flowers.

- Wicker baskets make charming containers for flowers.

Fill the bottle tops with air-drying clay, then push the foliage stems into place. Start with a basic structure, then fill in with choice blooms according to the final shape that you are trying to achieve. For a basket or 'countryside' arrangement, add a little 'moss' around the edge

△ Upstairs in the country store is a flower arrangement business. These types of arrangements are enjoyable to make and can be placed in the dolls' house as well as the shop.

of the container to disguise it. Use braid to decorate a plain pot.

Principles of design
Use the same ideas in miniature as in full-size arrangements. Use foliage as a skeleton structure and add your larger blooms before filling in with smaller ones. Miniature flower arrangements work well when you use plenty of blooms.

General store

A general store is perfect for displaying all sorts of household items from brushes and buckets to knives and knitting needles. Collect baskets and make simple boxes to act as containers.

A photograph taken in the 1920s of a real village general store inspired this miniature version. The window display uses a mixture of bought and hand-made items. Keep any small pictures of products found in adverts to stick onto balsa wood boxes and dowel 'tins'. Use the top of bay windows as additional display areas

Easy-to-make items

Make a hanging rack by suspending a short length of bamboo skewer from two pieces of jewellery chain. Make 'S' hooks from thin wire and suspend jugs, buckets and pans from them.

Bind up pairs of headed pins to make knitting needles.

Cut up matchsticks to provide kindling. Wrap each bundle with a length of crochet thread.

Pad the bottom of rough cloth sacks with paper, then fill with chunks of barbecue coal.

Twist newspaper into 4in (102mm) 'sausages'; put layers of newspaper soaked in wallpaper paste over the top, to form 'meat carcasses'. When dry, paint with acrylic paint (using pictures of butchered meat as reference), then varnish. Tie the limbs with crochet thread and suspend from hooks.

Cut a 1in (25mm) length of cocktail stick and tie very short lengths of crochet thread to one end to form washing-up brushes.

Shape blocks of balsa wood into barrel shapes. Paint dark brown and varnish.

Use toothbrush heads to make broom heads and scrubbing brushes.

Something different

The enjoyment of the miniatures hobby
extends beyond decorating and filling
rooms in the dolls' house, and there are
lots of individual projects and scenes that
you can try without having to commit
yourself to a whole house. You can also
make some unusual presents for your
friends and family to enjoy.

Arabian tent

This is an unconventional miniature house. Experimenting with mosaic glass tiles created the flooring, and a variety of bright, silky fabrics provide an exotic look for the tent and the many cushions

You will need:

- 12in (305mm) square MDF for the base
- Mosaic glass tiles (or tiled paper)
- 4 four-poster bed posts
- ½ x ¼in (13 x 6mm) stripwood
- ⅜in (10mm) square wood moulding
- ½ x ¼ in (13 x 6mm) wood moulding
- ⅛in (3mm) stripwood
- Fancy edging (gable trim)
- PVA glue
- Glue gun (optional)
- Cocktail sticks
- Fabrics
- Gold spray paint

To make the base

1 If you are using mosaic tiles, mark a 9in (229mm) square on the centre of the MDF base, then decide on a mosaic pattern by arranging the tiles on a piece of paper this size. If you don't wish to use real tiles use tiled-effect paper instead.

2 To help you to keep your tiling straight, bisect the MDF base with pencil lines to create a grid (Fig 1).

3 Then, start arranging the tiles in the centre of the base, using tile adhesive to secure them in place. Leave a small space between each tile for the grout, and leave a space in each corner for the tent post (Fig 2). (If your finished tiling creates a square with sides greater than 9in (229mm), adjust the measurements for the top bars of the tent structure and roof templates accordingly.)

4 When the tiles are set, grout between them, wiping off the excess. Set aside to dry while you make the tent structure.

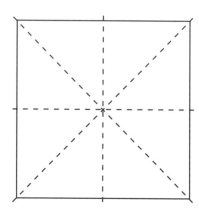

Fig 1 View from above

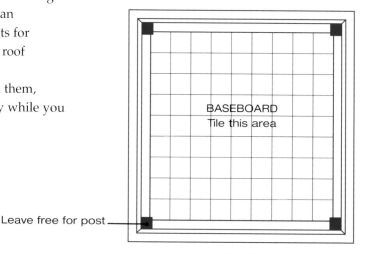

BASEBOARD
Tile this area

Leave free for post

Fig 2

To make the tent structure

1 Lengthen the four bed posts to 9in (229mm), using sections of square moulding. Use pegs cut from cocktail sticks to strengthen the butt joints (Fig 3) and insert these into the holes drilled in the centre of the posts and moulding.

2 Cut four top bars 8¼ in (209mm) long from the ½ x ¼ in (13 x 6mm) stripwood, and four lengths of fancy moulding (such as gingerbread gable trim). Join the top bars to the top of the posts, using peg joints to strengthen the butt joints. Turn the structure upside down on your workbench and glue the fancy trim beneath each top bar (Fig 4).

3 Spray the structure with gold paint – be careful, as everything will feel quite fragile.

4 When the structure is dry, glue the posts into the spaces left at the corners of the tiled floor. Again, you could use peg joints here.

5 Add lengths of ⅛ in (3mm) stripwood around each edge.

6 Use the template (Fig 5) to cut out the four triangles that form the roof.

7 Glue these together at the short edges and secure with masking tape to make a pyramid (Fig 6). Set this to one side until the fabric cover is ready.

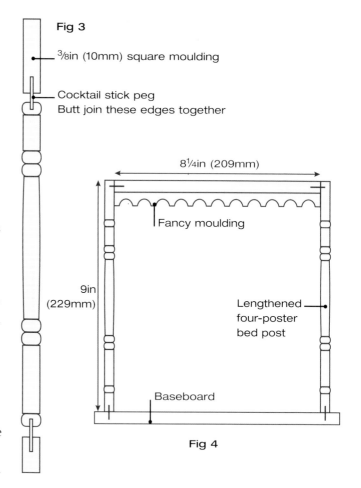

Fig 3

⅜in (10mm) square moulding

Cocktail stick peg
Butt join these edges together

8¼in (209mm)

Fancy moulding

9in
(229mm)

Lengthened four-poster bed post

Baseboard

Fig 4

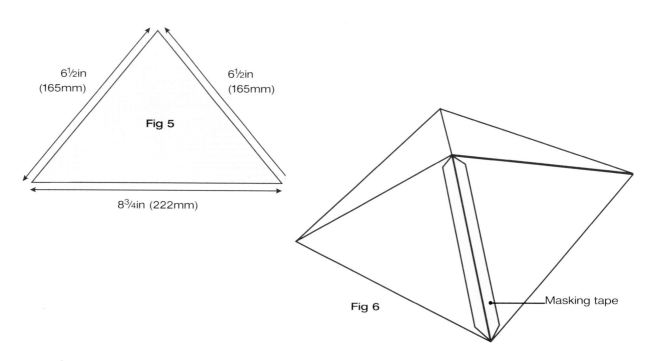

6½in (165mm)

6½in (165mm)

Fig 5

8¾in (222mm)

Fig 6

Masking tape

To make the fabric cover

1 If using pleated fabric for the tent ceiling, as I did, make this first, securing the pleats with interfacing.
2 Pin the roof template (Fig 5) to the ceiling fabric and cut out four triangles. Remember to add a seam allowance to each side (Fig 7).
3 With the right sides of the fabric facing, stitch the triangles together along the shorter edges, to make a floppy pyramid.
4 Glue the floppy pyramid to the inside of the card pyramid, securing the base edges with masking tape to the outside lower edge of the pyramid. Glue a jewel (e.g. a fake pearl earring) to the central point inside.

5 Glue the pyramid to the top of the tent structure (Fig 8). I used a glue gun.
6 Cut another four triangles from a second fabric for the outside of the roof, using the template (Fig 9).
7 Sew these together, with right sides facing, to make another floppy pyramid shape. Turn the right way out.
8 Next, make two proper walls and two shorter walls (Fig 10). Sew each colourway set together at the side seams, and slipstitch the two colours together at the outside edges. Rather than sew the fabric together at the bottom, I secured the

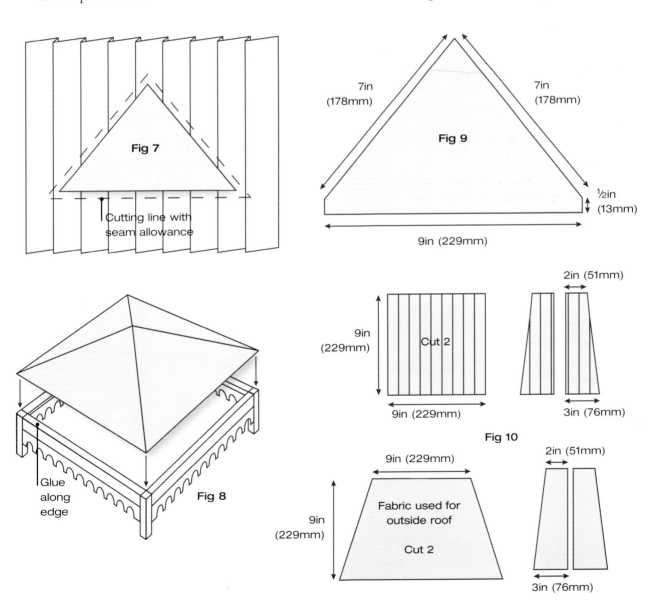

Fig 7

Cutting line with seam allowance

7in (178mm)   7in (178mm)

Fig 9

½in (13mm)

9in (229mm)

Glue along edge   Fig 8

2in (51mm)

9in (229mm)

Cut 2

9in (229mm)

3in (76mm)

Fig 10

9in (229mm)

2in (51mm)

9in (229mm)

Fabric used for outside roof

Cut 2

3in (76mm)

threads with liquid fabric sealant. This should make a long 'skirt' shape (Fig 11). Carefully pull the fabric cover over the tent structure.

9 Sew the raw edges at the top of the walls to the outside roof pyramid.

10 Decorate the tent with braid and beads.

11 Make guy ropes out of gold threads, and use these to secure the tent to shortened cocktail-stick tent pegs at the perimeter corners of the baseboard.

12 Fill the tent with accessories as your imagination dictates (see suggestions below).

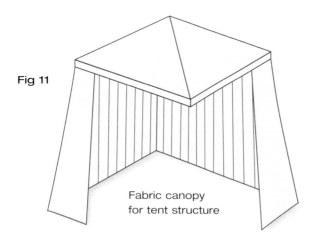

Fig 11

Fabric canopy
for tent structure

Accessories

Make dates from small balls of brown polymer clay rolled into the shape of mouse droppings. Push together into a plait. Bake and varnish when cooked and cold.

Cut squares of fabric for the cushions, sew two together and fill with rice grains until suitably squashy. Sew picot braid around the edges.

Use felt or fur fabric to create animal skin, and draw on markings with felt-tip pen.

Cut down corks for drums and stretch leather across the top.

Make a table like the one shown from sections of a fretwork fan, glued together with poly cement and sprayed gold.

Glue together large beads to make bottles and containers for oriental perfumes and spices.

Bandstand

A bandstand is a perfect place to display figures – either your own
creations, or the work of others.

To make the bandstand

You will need:

- 2 x ½in (13mm) thick hexagonal cake boards, 16in (406mm) across, point to point
- 1 x ½in (13mm) thick cake board, 9in (229mm) across, point to point
- Mountboard
- Thick polystyrene sheeting
- Masking tape
- Gummed paper tape
- Fancy stripwood
- 6 x 12in (305mm) lengths of ⅜in (10mm) dowel
- 5 large plastic railing pieces
- 6 small plastic railing pieces
- 6 large buttons and 4 decorative buttons
- Glue
- Gold spray paint
- Black, red, grey, gold acrylic paint
- Satin varnish
- Superglue

1 Draw around the cake board onto both the polystyrene sheet and a piece of mountboard, and cut out both shapes with a sharp knife.

2 Sandwich the polystyrene between the two large cake boards and tape the three layers together.

3 Mark the positions for the dowel pillars on the paper side of both cake boards, and carefully drill holes large enough to take the dowels. Make sure that you keep the drill bit vertical when you drill the base section.

4 To complete the base, tape the mountboard hexagon onto the bottom of the polystyrene.

5 Carefully push the six dowel lengths into the holes, and position the ceiling hexagon on top to check construction, then disassemble the components.

6 Paint the dowels with acrylic paint to suit, and varnish when dry.

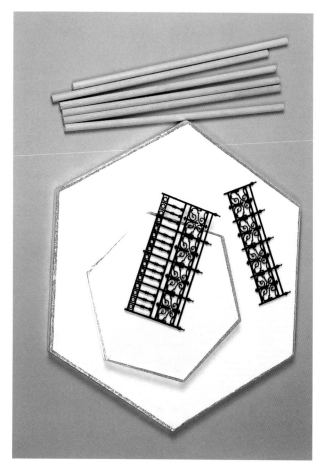

7 Cut six pieces of the fancy stripwood to fit around the base of the smaller cake board. Centre this on the top of the large hexagon and glue into place.

8 Cover each drilled hole on the top hexagon with a fancy button, having first removed any shanks with a saw.

9 Glue the base parts of the bandstand together with PVA glue, and wrap gummed paper strips around the sides, tucking under the base but not over the top. Either glue a strip of brick paper around the base, or paint it.

10 Glue the dowels in place on the thick base of the bandstand. When dry, add the top cake board.

11 Glue the railings between the dowels, the large section against the bottom and the smaller section against the top. If necessary, trim some of the plastic pegs on the railings with a sharp knife, then use Superglue to secure the railings in place.

12 As a finishing touch, add some decorative buttons around the base, and a set of steps.

▷ These plastic railings have been sprayed with gold paint to make them more attractive; masking tape was used to cover up the areas to be left black. Remember to spray each side of the railings, and always spray in the open air, to disseminate the fumes.

Theatre box

A tiered theatre box full of characters can tell a story. This scene is set in Edwardian England in the heyday of the music hall, with its mixture of songs, magic and comics acts. But you could adapt the idea for ballet fans, or a pantomime crowd. If you enjoy making or collecting miniature dolls, this provides an amusing setting to contain them.

You will need:

Make the box from ¼in (6mm) MDF:
- Left side: 3¾ x 24¾in (95 x 629mm)
- Right side: 6¼ x 24¾in (158 x 629mm)
- 2 floors: cut each from a piece 11¼ x 6½in (285 x 165mm), shape front edge
- Top: cut from a piece 11¼ x 6½in (285 x 165mm), shape front edge
- Bottom: cut from a piece 11¼ x 6½in (285 x 165mm), shape front edge
- Back: 11¼ x 24¾in (285 x 629mm)

- Cornice moulding
- Wood glue and PVA
- Wallpaper – plain and textured
- Braid and trimming
- Jewellery findings
- Self-adhesive carpet
- Sheet timber
- Wood beading
- Wood sheeting
- Corrugated card
- Mountboard

1 Shape the front edges of the top, bottom and floors as in the diagram.
2 Glue the box together, leaving the floors until last. Remember that the sides and back panel sit on top of the base, and the top sits on the sides and back panel.
3 Decorate the interior walls with wallpaper, leaving narrow gaps for the cornices. Paint the cornices and glue them in place, equally spaced on both internal sides, and the back of the box.
4 Decorate the floors before you slide them into place. Paint the underneath with emulsion paint and apply self-adhesive carpet to the top.
5 Make three false doors, each 6½ x 3in (165 x 76mm), from wood sheeting. Use wood moulding to make a doorframe. In this model the lowest tier is shown with the door open. The false door is glued at an angle, and the doorway is painted black.
6 Make the front walls from a double skin of corrugated card, 3⅛in (79mm) wide, with the vertical ribs turned to the inside, and supported internally at intervals with lengths of ½in (13mm) stripwood.
7 Glue the front curved wall securely to each floor and against the sides. Decorate with wallpaper and top with a shaped piece of mountboard covered with self-adhesive carpet.
8 Spray sections of textured wallpaper with gold paint and glue to each external side. Decorate the fronts of the theatre box with jewellery findings.

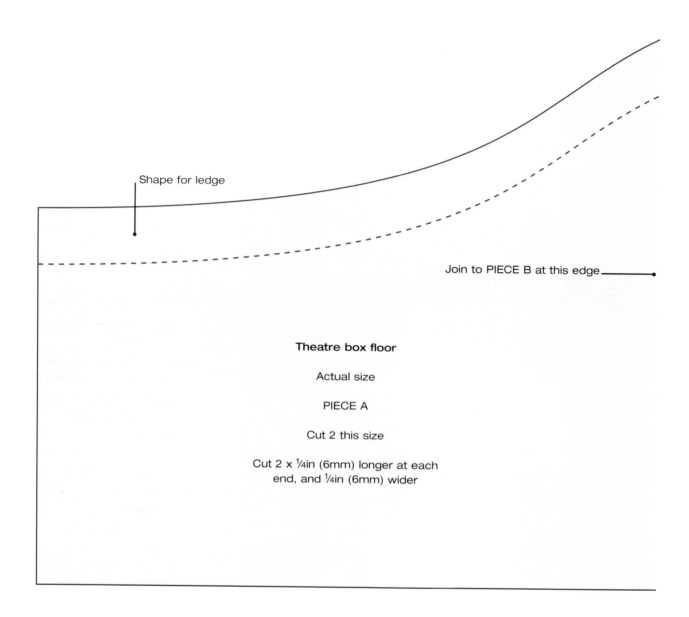

Shape for ledge

Join to PIECE B at this edge

Theatre box floor

Actual size

PIECE A

Cut 2 this size

Cut 2 x ¼in (6mm) longer at each
end, and ¼in (6mm) wider

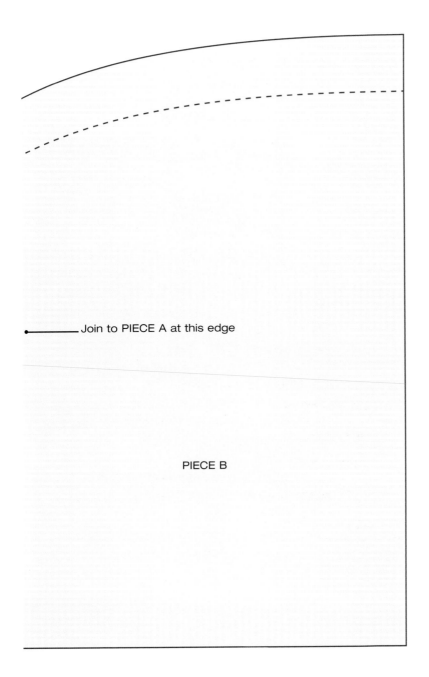

Join to PIECE A at this edge

PIECE B

To complete the theatre box you can add curtains, programmes, and personal effects such as bags and chocolate boxes. Framed theatre posters liven up the walls. Look through books on the history of theatre for samples. Photocopy and reduce in size, before covering with a thin sheet of plastic and edging with painted stripwood. If you have access to a computer you can create your own posters.

Lights have been installed in my theatre box but this is optional, and they do not have to be working examples.

This audience is sitting on wirework seats, sprayed gold. I used 12 seats in all but, as they are hardly seen, you could always perch each person on a block of wood or film canister. You could make your own audience from polymer clay – the Edwardian era provides a good opportunity for creating wonderful hats, fans, and bags.

Polymer clay people

There can be few people who haven't made figures out of pipe cleaners. These rudimentary skeletons are the basis for dolls' house people, but achieving the right scale is essential.

Draw out a basic chart on a piece of paper so that you can check your figure as you proceed.

A 1:12 scale adult man will need to be about 6in (152mm) tall, a woman is a little shorter at around 5½in (140mm), and a child even shorter still depending upon 'age'.

To make a person

You will need:
- Pipe cleaners (any colour)
- Toy stuffing
- Stretchy white material (old T-shirts are ideal)
- Flesh-coloured polymer clay
- Cocktail stick
- Scalpel
- Skewer

If this is your first attempt, don't worry about gender, but make sure you keep a height chart beside you as you work. Begin with the arms, as these are easier than the head and face and will give you confidence.

Making perfect people takes practice, so don't let your first attempt deter you. When I started making people I found it was easier to make male figures. Not being skilled at shaping the polymer clay, I found the blocky appearance of the heads and hands I made better suited to male dolls. Women are more rounded, and smoother, while children are generally smaller all over. Over time I have perfected my dolls and they certainly have a distinctive look – all part of the same family that's for sure!

◁ This Victorian man is dressed in a formal suit. Remember that you only need to make the parts of clothing that will be seen.

Working with polymer clay
As with any clay project, there are basic rules. Your work surface should be clean and flat – a melamine place mat is ideal. Keep your hands clean to avoid making the clay grubby when you knead it and avoid using old stock, as aging polymer clay is crumbly and difficult to work.

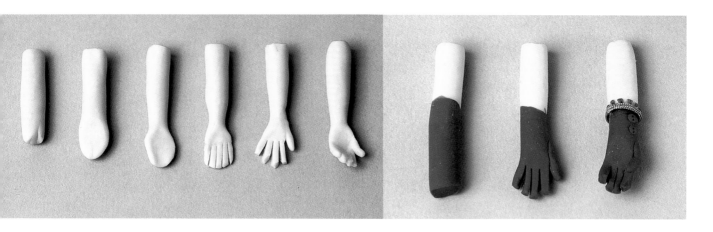

To make the arms and hands

1 To make the arms, take a piece of polymer clay and roll it into a sausage shape about ¼in (6mm) in diameter.

2 Cut a section to the lower arm length and push a skewer into one end to make a hole.

3 Flatten the other end of the arm to form a paddle shape. Gently smooth over any cracks that appear.

4 Roll the clay limb gently between your two index fingers to form a wrist. It only needs a couple of rolls.

5 Place the limb on a smooth surface and cut four lines with a scalpel, halfway down the paddle, to create the fingers.

6 Cut through the last line completely – this will be the thumb. Gently re-shape the removed piece and stick it back on a little lower down the palm, in the thumb position. Use the cocktail stick to smooth the join.

7 Trim and shape all the fingers carefully to correct their lengths and separate slightly. If cracks appear, smooth as necessary.

8 Gently push the rounded end of a paintbrush into the palm of the clay hand to define the area. If you intend your dolls to hold an object, gently curl the fingers appropriately.

9 Make a second arm in the same fashion, but remember to put the thumb on the other side of the palm.

△ If you want your figure to wear gloves, blend another colour clay onto a stub of flesh tone and follow the above instructions, although the fingers do not need to be as well rounded. Add buttons and a picot trim after baking.

▽ The young boy holds a diabolo and his fingers have been carefully curved prior to baking to accommodate the toy.

To make the legs and feet

1 The shoes are moulded as part of the limb and painted after baking.

2 Take a sausage of flesh-coloured clay and roll a little thicker than the arm.

3 Make a hole in one end and bend the other carefully to form the foot.

4 Shape the foot into a shoe. Rounding the toe and heel. For a woman's heel, stand the foot on the handle of your scalpel as it lies on your work surface; push the toe down to that surface. Lift the shoe away. Shape a small stump of clay and add it carefully to form the heel. Make small clay buttons up the side for women's boots.

5 Make a matching shoe and bake according to the manufacturer's instructions.

6 When cold, holding the leg on a cocktail stick, paint the shoe area with acrylic paint. Paint in socks or stockings and varnish when dry.

When you have completed the limbs you should feel more confident about shaping the clay. Heads and faces will need practice, so don't feel too disheartened at your first attempt.

Once you have the arms and legs attempt the head. Men's heads are good to start with, as they can be quite rugged.

△ The legs on this little girl are hidden by the dress, so don't have to be too neat in their construction. She is, however, wearing pantaloons beneath the dress.

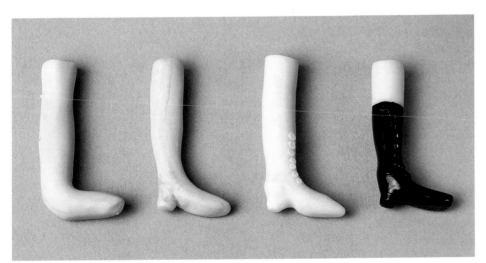

◁ The shoes are moulded as part of the limb and painted on after baking. Men's legs are easier to shape. The heel of a woman's shoe needs a little practice to get right.

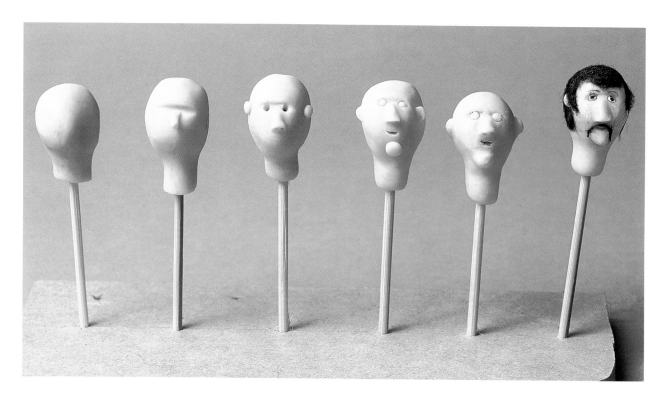

To make the head

1 Start with a ¾in (19mm) ball of clay and roll it into an egg shape. Push the clay a little, so that there is more at the front, and roll one end to create a neck.
2 Make a hole in the neck, so that the finished head can be inserted onto the pipe cleaner skeleton. Make sure that it reaches up inside the 'skull', almost to the cranium.
3 At eye level make a dent with the edge of the scalpel handle. In the middle of this dent and just below it, add a small sausage of clay – this will become the nose.
4 Smooth and shape the nose against the face, using the sides of the cocktail stick, and the point to make the nostrils.
5 Use a cocktail stick to shape two eye sockets. Circle the holes slightly so that they become more cone-like than tubular in shape. Roll two tiny balls of clay and push these into the eye sockets.
6 Add two pieces of clay for the ears, if they are likely to be seen on the finished doll and not hidden by hair. Flatten the edges with the cocktail stick to blend the join.

7 To define the chin, blend in a small ball of clay. If you don't like the effect, smooth the area over and start again.
8 Form a mouth opening with the scalpel.

An adult female head should be smaller and more rounded, than a man's head. Children's heads are smaller still, and can be almost like buttons. If you don't like the head, you can always squash it together and start again but, once you are happy with the face that you have created, bake it following the instructions on the polymer clay packet.

I use acrylic paint for the eye and lip detail when painting the face. A little wash of pink or red may be rubbed over the cheek or chin. Style your dolls' hair and glue it into place. For women glue a small bead to each ear to represent an earring.

Constructing the figure

1 Push the limbs onto the pipe cleaners to check their length, trimming the pipe cleaner where necessary. If the limbs seem out of proportion, you can saw through the clay to make them shorter, but do this carefully.

2 Glue the limbs in place. The figure will look fairly odd at this stage.

3 Wrap toy stuffing around the skeleton to define the flesh, adding more in appropriate areas such as bosoms, bellies and bottoms.

4 Cut a rectangular piece of old T-shirt and sew it around the torso with the seam at the back. Cut a couple of slits to get the fabric under the arms. Sew it over the shoulders. You can also repeat this process for the arms and legs, though often the clothing is enough to secure the stuffing. Alternatively, wind sewing thread up the limbs to hold the stuffing. Your figure will now look as though it is wearing long johns and is ready for dressing as you wish.

▽ As you dress your doll you can always push extra stuffing into the trouser legs or down the arms if your initial skeleton is a bit skinny.

Tips

There are several books that go into great detail about making and dressing dolls' for the dolls' house. When you follow a clothing pattern always make a template out of kitchen paper first to check the fit, as home-made dolls such as mine are unlikely to have the perfect proportions of porcelain ones bought from professional makers.

When it comes to dressing the dolls, you need only make the parts of clothes that show – men's collars and shirt fronts, for example, as the clothing is not made to be removable. Seal cut edges with liquid fabric sealant to stop fabric from fraying – easier than making tiny hems on garments.

Make sure that you choose clothing fabric carefully, natural fibres are best. Look for small patterns or use plain fabric to keep the illusion of scale. There are specialist dolls' house haberdashers who can supply appropriate materials.

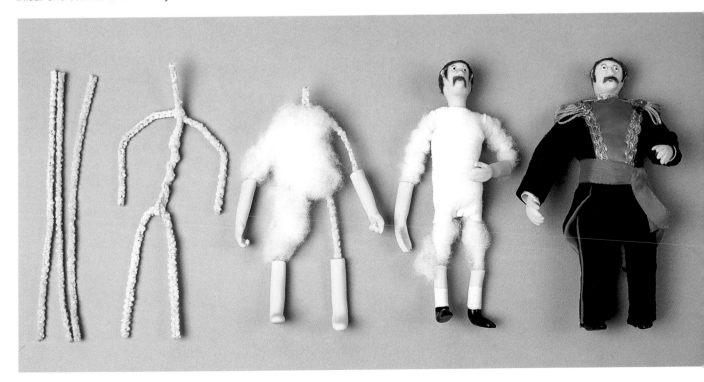

Boxed up and ready to go

You don't have to use a conventional frame box to display a miniature scene. Many boxes are suitable and can make excellent and unique gifts. With a little imagination, the new contents can reflect the original purpose of the container.

Biscuit box

A cylindrical biscuit box or whisky tube can be recycled into a personal gift. Carefully cut out a rectangle from one side. Glue in a circular base of card resting on a block of balsa wood – or a rolled up strip of corrugated card – level with the opening that you have cut. Add curved shelves or floors made from mountboard higher up, as desired, and support these on narrow strips of card slightly curled to fit against the curve of the container.

◁ This is perfect as a holiday souvenir as it lasts longer than the original contents of the tin. Refer back to the shop projects for cakes, sweets and biscuits.

Wine box

Many wine boxes come complete with a convenient carrying handle. Simply open the box and remove the internal bag (having drunk the wine). Cut out a section from the back panel (to retain the illusion from the front of the box of its original use) and decorate as you would a small room box.

▷ Mirror tiles are perfect behind this cocktail bar. The bar itself is made out of corrugated card, as it curves easily, and faced with art paper that has been sprayed silver.

Gift boxes

Even the conventional gift box can be dressed up with miniature items to personalize them. You can make or buy the selection to go on top of the box. Simply glue them firmly in place. If you have any paper items, such as sheet music, tiny magazine covers, playing cards, etc, make sure that these are glued in place before the larger items.

Clock

Clocks are easy to make, and can be personalized or given a theme to make a suitable gift. They also make ideal projects for dolls' house clubs.

Clock mechanisms are readily available through craft shops. Check that the clock hands and mechanism are compatible. Make sure your MDF is large enough to accommodate the hands – the length of the clock spindle will determine the thickness of the MDF that you need.

Make your own miniatures, or use commercially available pieces to represent the numbers.

You will need:
- Clock mechanism and hands
- A rectangle of MDF (or commercial clock blank)
- A selection of miniatures to go around the dial
- Brick-effect wallpaper
- Hobby spray varnish
- Paint
- PVA glue
- Superglue
- Wood glue
- Stripwood, 1in (25mm) square
- A mirror plate

The basic clock
1 The longest clock hand (minute or second) will help determine the size of your clock face.
2 Draw a circle with a radius equal to the longest clock hand to make a paper template for your dial.
3 Use this as a guide when cutting the MDF. Drill a suitable hole to take the clock mechanism.
4 Glue stripwood (equal to the depth of your clock mechanism) around the back.

▷ Buy a simple clock mechanism at a craft shop or hobby store.

THERE IS ALWAYS TIME FOR MINIATURES

Decorating the clock

1 Paint your clock face in a colour of your choice (I used emulsion paint).
2 Cover the sides in brick-effect wallpaper.
3 Print out the phrase 'there is always time for miniatures' on a computer, or use rubdown transfer lettering (or letters cut from a magazine).
4 Cut each letter out and arrange around a circle of white paper, spacing each as required.
5 Glue each letter in place, then photocopy onto coloured paper.
6 Cut a small hole in the centre of the paper circle and line it up with the spindle hole. Glue in place.

Adding the numbers

1 Decide where you want each miniature to be placed around the dial.
2 Glue any paper-thin miniatures (newspaper, sheet music, magazine covers, etc) on first. Varnish over the face twice, allowing the first coat to dry before applying the second.
3 Stick the remaining miniatures in place. Use Superglue for heavy items (although these are best avoided). Make sure that their position does not interfere with the rotation of the clock hands.

Finishing off

1 Spray the clock face again with varnish, preferably in the open air. Several light coats are better than one thick one. Leave to dry.
2 Attach a mirror plate to the centre back to hang it on the wall.
3 Attach the clock mechanism and the clock hands.
4 Insert an appropriate battery and enjoy watching time slip by.

▷ Place your message around the clock face.

About the author

Growing up in a creative family, Christiane Berridge experimented with a variety of crafts including stencilling, patchwork and toy-making before discovering dolls' houses. Making miniatures is now a way of life for her.

With a BSc (Hons) in Geography, Christiane worked in a variety of jobs including countryside conservation and museum education, before landing the perfect position as editor of *The Dolls' House Magazine*. Now she enjoys encouraging all aspects of the miniatures hobby as well as exploring new ideas from unusual sources.

Despite the demands of a busy household (husband and three children) Christiane still finds the time to make items for her own dolls' houses, as well as larger accessories for local opera and music groups, where she has contributed to 37 shows in the last six years.

Dolls' houses remain an absolute passion and imaginative ideas are always at Christiane's fingertips. This, her first book, contains just a few of them.

Index

WOODCARVING

Beginning Woodcarving — *GMC Publications*
Carving Architectural Detail in Wood: The Classical Tradition — *Frederick Wilbur*
Carving Birds & Beasts — *GMC Publications*
Carving the Human Figure: Studies in Wood and Stone — *Dick Onians*
Carving Nature: Wildlife Studies in Wood — *Frank Fox-Wilson*
Carving on Turning — *Chris Pye*
Celtic Carved Lovespoons: 30 Patterns — *Sharon Littley & Clive Griffin*
Decorative Woodcarving (New Edition) — *Jeremy Williams*
Elements of Woodcarving — *Chris Pye*
Essential Woodcarving Techniques — *Dick Onians*
Lettercarving in Wood: A Practical Course — *Chris Pye*
Relief Carving in Wood: A Practical Introduction — *Chris Pye*
Woodcarving for Beginners — *GMC Publications*
Woodcarving Tools, Materials & Equipment — *Chris Pye*

WOODWORKING

Beginning Picture Marquetry — *Lawrence Threadgold*
Celtic Carved Lovespoons: 30 Patterns — *Sharon Littley & Clive Griffin*
Celtic Woodcraft — *Glenda Bennett*
Complete Woodfinishing (Revised Edition) — *Ian Hosker*
David Charlesworth's Furniture-Making Techniques — *David Charlesworth*
David Charlesworth's Furniture-Making Techniques – Volume 2 — *David Charlesworth*
Furniture-Making Projects for the Wood Craftsman — *GMC Publications*
Furniture-Making Techniques for the Wood Craftsman — *GMC Publications*
Furniture Projects with the Router — *Kevin Ley*
Furniture Restoration (Practical Crafts) — *Kevin Jan Bonner*
Furniture Restoration: A Professional at Work — *John Lloyd*
Furniture Restoration and Repair for Beginners — *Kevin Jan Bonner*
Furniture Restoration Workshop — *Kevin Jan Bonner*
Green Woodwork — *Mike Abbott*
Intarsia: 30 Patterns for the Scrollsaw — *John Everett*
Kevin Ley's Furniture Projects — *Kevin Ley*
Making Chairs and Tables – Volume 2 — *GMC Publications*
Making Classic English Furniture — *Paul Richardson*
Making Heirloom Boxes — *Peter Lloyd*
Making Screw Threads in Wood — *Fred Holder*
Making Woodwork Aids and Devices — *Robert Wearing*
Mastering the Router — *Ron Fox*
Pine Furniture Projects for the Home — *Dave Mackenzie*
Router Magic: Jigs, Fixtures and Tricks to Unleash your Router's Full Potential — *Bill Hylton*
Router Projects for the Home — *GMC Publications*
Router Tips & Techniques — *Robert Wearing*
Routing: A Workshop Handbook — *Anthony Bailey*
Routing for Beginners — *Anthony Bailey*
Sharpening: The Complete Guide — *Jim Kingshott*
Space-Saving Furniture Projects — *Dave Mackenzie*
Stickmaking: A Complete Course — *Andrew Jones & Clive George*
Stickmaking Handbook — *Andrew Jones & Clive George*
Storage Projects for the Router — *GMC Publications*
Veneering: A Complete Course — *Ian Hosker*
Veneering Handbook — *Ian Hosker*
Woodworking Techniques and Projects — *Anthony Bailey*
Woodworking with the Router: Professional Router Techniques any Woodworker can Use — *Bill Hylton & Fred Matlack*

UPHOLSTERY

Upholstery: A Complete Course (Revised Edition) — *David James*
Upholstery Restoration — *David James*
Upholstery Techniques & Projects — *David James*
Upholstery Tips and Hints — *David James*

TOYMAKING

Scrollsaw Toy Projects — *Ivor Carlyle*
Scrollsaw Toys for All Ages — *Ivor Carlyle*

GARDENING

Alpine Gardening — *Chris & Valerie Wheeler*
Auriculas for Everyone: How to Grow and Show Perfect Plants — *Mary Robinson*
Beginners' Guide to Herb Gardening — *Yvonne Cuthbertson*
Beginners' Guide to Water Gardening — *Graham Clarke*
The Birdwatcher's Garden — *Hazel & Pamela Johnson*
Companions to Clematis: Growing Clematis with Other Plants — *Marigold Badcock*
Creating Contrast with Dark Plants — *Freya Martin*
Creating Small Habitats for Wildlife in your Garden — *Josie Briggs*
Exotics are Easy — *GMC Publications*
Gardening with Hebes — *Chris & Valerie Wheeler*
Gardening with Wild Plants — *Julian Slatcher*
Growing Cacti and Other Succulents in the Conservatory and Indoors — *Shirley-Anne Bell*
Growing Cacti and Other Succulents in the Garden — *Shirley-Anne Bell*
Growing Successful Orchids in the Greenhouse and Conservatory — *Mark Isaac-Williams*
Hardy Palms and Palm-Like Plants — *Martyn Graham*
Hardy Perennials: A Beginner's Guide — *Eric Sawford*
Hedges: Creating Screens and Edges — *Averil Bedrich*
Marginal Plants — *Bernard Sleeman*
Orchids are Easy: A Beginner's Guide to their Care and Cultivation — *Tom Gilland*
Plant Alert: A Garden Guide for Parents — *Catherine Collins*
Planting Plans for Your Garden — *Jenny Shukman*
Sink and Container Gardening Using Dwarf Hardy Plants — *Chris & Valerie Wheeler*
The Successful Conservatory and Growing Exotic Plants — *Joan Phelan*
Tropical Garden Style with Hardy Plants — *Alan Hemsley*
Water Garden Projects: From Groundwork to Planting — *Roger Sweetinburgh*

ART TECHNIQUES

Oil Paintings from your Garden: A Guide for Beginners

Rachel Shirley

VIDEOS

Drop-in and Pinstuffed Seats	*David James*
Stuffover Upholstery	*David James*
Elliptical Turning	*David Springett*
Woodturning Wizardry	*David Springett*
Turning Between Centres: The Basics	*Dennis White*
Turning Bowls	*Dennis White*
Boxes, Goblets and Screw Threads	*Dennis White*

Novelties and Projects	*Dennis White*
Classic Profiles	*Dennis White*
Twists and Advanced Turning	*Dennis White*
Sharpening the Professional Way	*Jim Kingshott*
Sharpening Turning & Carving Tools	*Jim Kingshott*
Bowl Turning	*John Jordan*
Hollow Turning	*John Jordan*
Woodturning: A Foundation Course	*Keith Rowley*
Carving a Figure: The Female Form	*Ray Gonzalez*
The Router: A Beginner's Guide	*Alan Goodsell*
The Scroll Saw: A Beginner's Guide	*John Burke*

MAGAZINES

WOODTURNING ✦ WOODCARVING ✦ FURNITURE & CABINETMAKING
THE ROUTER ✦ NEW WOODWORKING ✦ THE DOLLS' HOUSE MAGAZINE
OUTDOOR PHOTOGRAPHY ✦ BLACK & WHITE PHOTOGRAPHY
TRAVEL PHOTOGRAPHY ✦ MACHINE KNITTING NEWS
GUILD OF MASTER CRAFTSMEN NEWS

The above represents a selection of titles currently published or scheduled to be published.
All are available direct from the Publishers or through bookshops, newsagents and specialist retailers.
To place an order, or to obtain a complete catalogue, contact:

GMC Publications,
Castle Place, 166 High Street, Lewes, East Sussex BN7 1XU United Kingdom
Tel: 01273 488005 Fax: 01273 402866
E-mail: pubs@thegmcgroup.com

Orders by credit card are accepted

Acknowledgements

This book wouldn't have been possible without the support and encouragement
of others. These include Joyce Dean, who nursed me through my early days of
dolls' house journalism; fellow enthusiasts Pat King and Jean Nisbett who
shared their words of wisdom; GMC, who allowed me to present my projects
through *The Dolls' House Magazine*; my editor, Gill Parris, whose patience
ensured this book became a reality; Anthony Bailey and Gilda Pacitti, who have
presented my projects in print with such skill.

Finally, a huge thank you to my family, Paul, Edward, Eleanor and Toby Berridge,
for accepting the time spent on writing this book without complaining.